Recollections of a Path Maker

STEPPING STONES

an autobiographical journey with
Alice Frampton Dittman

as told to and authored by
Mary Potter Schwaner

PRAIRIE MUSE BOOKS INC
LINCOLN, NEBRASKA
©2021

STEPPING STONES
Copyright © 2021 by Alice Frampton Dittman
IngramSpark Print Edition HQ
ISBN978-1-952911-29-3

Contact booklady@maryschwaner.com
Cover design by Prairie Muse utilizing photo
by Craig Chandler, UNL Office of Communications
Use only with permission.

Dedication

I'm forever grateful to those who laid the stepping stones that led me to make inroads in the banking industry as a woman. My parents—Cecile and George Frampton— are chief among them.

My greatest pride now rests in the many who have stepped through those opening doors and made even further improvements in the banking arena which I have loved and actively participated in for seventy years. If they know me at all, they know how thoroughly I support and respect their successes.

~Alice Marilyn Frampton Dittman

PRINCES *and* KINGS

Isn't it strange how princes and kings,
and clowns that caper in sawdust rings,
and common people, like you and me,
are builders for eternity?

Each is given a list of rules;
a shapeless mass; a bag of tools.
And each must fashion, ere life is flown,
a stumbling block, or a stepping-stone.

R. LEE SHARPE

A Word From Alice

This book is about so many things in my lifetime—
and my family's. It is also about all the co-workers
who helped make so many good things happen at
Cornhusker Bank.

Perhaps it is too long, but it is written from my heart
and with great appreciation for the years of service.

May you *all* who read this—in 2021 and beyond—
share the joy of helping others attain *their* dreams.

Fondly,

Alice

P.S. I have just completed my 91st birthday
on October 1st, 2021!

One

I remember with clarity the day I put my tennis racket away for the last time. It had been a welcome fixture in my life as long as I can remember, but now my aging bones recoiled at the thought of giving my trusty racket one more outing. How was that possible?

At eighty-four years of age I hadn't just been shuffling around the court. I'd been playing real tennis. Even Seniors' singles tournaments. And winning. Sometimes. How was my mind going to deal with the fact that this vibrant aspect of my life was going to just... end?

Tennis kept me young. Tennis kept my reactions, my reflexes, sharp. Tennis kept me smiling when I could relegate some young whippersnapper to his or her proper place.

Truthfully, though, while winning was often my objective, I did take great pleasure in watching my opponent improve his or her game. My delight doubled if that person was a grandchild of mine. Now, however, letting someone else reign on the court was my best option. I still had my ping pong.

As I write this, six years after retiring my racket, I find myself comfortably moved into my 'retirement' apartment at The Landing.

There's plenty of room around the ping pong table for my grandkids.

The new lifestyle took some getting used to, and the medical issues I'd been battling did bring me low on occasion. Some years ago I'd had a heavy dose of radiation treatments—5,000 Rads, and more recently 5,000 more. As a result, some time ago my jawbone began to disintegrate. Literally. My speech disappointed me and words sometimes just slid away. Those who could understand my words were patient and reassuring. It was a stressful time.

Though it took a lot longer than I'd hoped, a seven-hour surgery with two surgeons and a new titanium jaw put things back in order. Mostly. But life is good. Issues resolve as best they can. And until Covid-19 struck in 2020, I was relatively free.

Covid-19 is a wicked virus unleashed in China that quickly spread across the world. It has been a true global pandemic. Young and old alike know well enough the damage it has wrought. Once the Covid pandemic got into full swing, much of Lincoln—including my residence, The Landing—was locked up. Masks were constantly in place and nonresident visitors were kept at bay. Quarantines have been stringent and caretakers vigilant. In the midst of all that, I was able to take a number of opportunities to leave my lodgings, and at this writing have still evaded the dreaded virus.

It has been difficult to see the damage that a country-wide—indeed, worldwide—shutdown is wreaking. Businesses we'd come to know through Cornhusker Bank were suffering with all the new restrictions. A business was to keep their customers six and a half feet apart; they were to sanitize after each customer, and allow only 50% or less of their usual capacity to be occupying the premises at one time. Restaurants innovated with take-away meals, and with ingenuity, businesses found ways to survive.

Covid-19 did its best to stifle our movements, and much as we longed for former freedoms, our Landing community has done a good job of complying with the rules. Sadly, as of this writing more than a year later, we have lost two residents.

It might surprise you to know, then, that in the midst of my desire to limit my home confinement, there was one unexpected happening that managed to keep me happily in my apartment.

In the days surrounding my 90th birthday, cards and letters began to spill into my mailbox. They crowded out the usual advertising clutter and gave me an unexpected eagerness to greet the postman. As I read the greetings, each written word seemed to launch its own contribution to a growing string of memories. Friends, colleagues, neighbors old and new, school chums and the like were phoning or dropping me a line to marvel at the fact that I was ninety years old and still kicking. On the day of my birthday, October 1st of 2020, a number of masked friends joined my family and me for a light dinner at *The Hub*, my son Doug's restaurant located near the campus of UNL. My daughter Dawn Dittman Coronado was quarantined in Austin, Texas, along with her husband Jim and my grandson Carson. They attended the event via Zoom on their computers.

As I read and re-read those wonderful birthday cards, a ribbon of warm recollection began to emerge. I truly hadn't expected that I'd get quite so hooked on it.

I read each word with surprise, many times more than once. With each reading, the sentiments became more and more humbling.

As I carefully laid them in my special orange box—the one my son John rounded up for me—I thought of the connections. A lifetime of drawing or being drawn, often with perfect strangers, into a welcoming circle, and then giving them the support they needed to join their strengths in a common effort. Whether in the bank or in the community, forming those kinds of connections for people has been one of my greatest sources of satisfaction. If it's a win for them, then it's a most gratifying win for me, and for the bank. Now the evidence of those connections has filled my orange box with over three hundred happy messages.

In my life I've been bolstered by the chance meetings that have forged enduring connections for me, for my family, and for Cornhusker Bank. I've been pleased when connections we have orchestrated between bank customers, associates, family and friends seem to grow into something special.

Banking has been my passion in life—the skill-building, the challenges met, the goals exceeded, and the mistakes overcome. Throughout, I've found it's the connections that have worked for me.

I don't recall ever having been pushed to establish connections with folks. My upbringing in Lincoln, Nebraska, was open and friendly. From my earliest days I felt free to explore whatever relationship worked with the people who came my way, and in doing that, I found pathways to new associations with people.

As a youngster, it was always just some simple thing that would draw my attention, like the folded bills and shiny coins that would spill from my father's pockets onto the hall table when he arrived home in the evening. Before long, I was counting it, and most evenings there would be another random sampling. My parents taught me well, and bit by bit I was unwittingly cementing a new connection.

That small exercise led to my wish to have a bit of money of my own, and soon my father made me a proposition. He offered to buy me a case of soda pop at 5¢ a bottle to get me started. All I had to do was find people to buy it from me. I thought that sounded good, so I immediately agreed. The next day he ordered a whole case of twenty-four glass bottles of soda. I piled them into my little red wagon, surrounded them with ice, and off I went. Up and down the neighborhood around 33rd Street I trudged, pulling that wagon. I peddled the pop for 10¢ a bottle—which seemed reasonable since I was doing all the work of bringing it right to peoples' doors—and within a day or two all of the soda pop was sold. And I was allowed to keep the money. When I counted up the receipts, I had enough to buy another case of pop, and my entrepreneurial self was born.

It was just great fun, that early lesson in commerce. And profitable, too. But there were other lessons, as well, like the time a fly dropped into a bottle and the entire bottle of soda had to be discarded. Such a disappointment that was. Perhaps that's when I learned to take it on the chin and keep moving forward.

I would have been about three years old in this photo

About three years of age with my father, George Frampton.
Taken at Waubonsie State Park in Hamburg, Iowa.

Two

There was nothing about that soda pop endeavor that felt like work. I think it was that way for my father, too, in his own career. From my earliest days, my father was involved either part-time or full-time in some form of the banking business. George Andrew Frampton had been born in Nebraska, near Louisville, but at age six, in the year 1901, his family left the state.

My father and his parents took a buckboard wagon south to participate in the last great land rush in Comanche County, Oklahoma, where they secured one-hundred-sixty acres to farm. It was here that George's older brother, my uncle Whispering John, broke horses. John was a big fellow with a booming voice that could be heard clear across the lake. Hence the nickname.

Thousands of people participated in that last land rush. I remember being told how my grandfather was waiting in line to draw a number that would put him in the lottery to compete for a parcel of land. But before he could draw a number, the farmer ahead of him fell over from heat exhaustion. My grandfather stepped out of line to help revive him, letting several people go past. When the man was recovered, my grandfather stepped back into the line. He might well have lost his chance at a good lottery number. However, as fortune would have it, he had landed in exactly the right spot, and the family was able to acquire a quarter section.

It was a bold time in our nation's history, and the Frampton family was a part of it. But their story didn't stop there.

When my grandfather, George H. Frampton, broke sod on his Oklahoma homestead in Comanche County, six miles south and three miles east of Cache, near Lawton, his plow blade struck metal. When he unearthed the buried object, it turned out to be a relic of the Spanish conquistadors—a metal twenty-five pound iron tether-weight engraved with an image of a Spanish knight. The weight has been dated to the 1500's. Some thought it was lost by the Coronado expedition, but I don't recall much more about it except to say that it later took up residence in Oklahoma's Museum of the Great Plains.

Farming wasn't an easy life, but it was sustainable. My dad's sister Ida and her husband Art Runyan stayed with the farm. Together they added many more quarter sections to the original homestead.

I'm sure it was those days that seated in Dad's mind the conviction that every family could be secure if there was at least one farmer among them. I know my son Doug would agree. He has inherited his great-grandparents' heart for farming and will be the first to quote my father saying, "Come the revolution, someone's got to farm."

Even so, nineteen-year-old George left the farm and returned to Nebraska, bent on studying business. He lived in the home of his uncle, Lincoln attorney Wm. Chariton Frampton, at 1602 E Street. The Lincoln School of Commerce provided the course work, and soon he secured his first bank employment in Denton, just southwest of Lincoln. To his great delight he was able to buy a brand new shotgun with his first paycheck. I would hear the joy in his voice when he recounted that bit of history. Each day he'd hop on the train that carried him back and forth from his lodgings in Lincoln and his work in Denton; slowly but surely the shape of his life's work began to emerge.

While my father never complained of it, he carried a lifelong scar from those years. A doctor was treating a few harmless moles on the back of Dad's hands, and managed to destroy the oil glands with the X-ray. My father paid the bill for the procedure, even though the doctor had burned his hands badly. Dad could never again grip tightly with his fingers, though it served him well in golf, where a light grip can be beneficial. For the rest of his life, daily small annoyances would crop up as a result of that debilitating encounter with 'modern' medical science.

Still, nothing about his appearance seemed anything but heroic to a certain young lady. Cecile Meyer was four years younger than George, and though she'd been raised on a farm near Mead, Nebraska, her family had relocated to Lincoln so that Cecile and her two sisters could enter college. What a remarkable thing that was! In those years, most young people never had the opportunity to roam the halls of higher learning. Many never even progressed past eighth grade in the early 1900's. But my mother's father, Nelson Meyer, a successful farmer, sold his land to move to Lincoln so his three daughters could attend college. It would have been unusual in those years for a man to do that, even for his sons. But for his daughters? Practically unheard of.

My mother was always an eager learner, so I'm quite sure Cecile thrived in college, both at Cotner College in Bethany and in her University of Nebraska Home Economics studies. Those were happy times. In 1918, George and Cecile married.

Cecile and George Frampton

Not long after their marriage, my mother and father left Lincoln. Perhaps it was a lingering connection with the Oklahoma homestead, but for whatever reason, my parents moved to Lawton, Oklahoma. My father worked in a bank there, and my mother taught piano lessons to the neighborhood children—when she wasn't working in the bank.

Soon their first child, George Frampton, Jr., was born. His sweet presence changed their lives, but within nine months they would experience the shattering sadness of losing him to what we now know as Sudden Infant Death Syndrome. The loss was devastating to the young couple.

For three years they threw themselves into organizing a new bank they were establishing in Faxson, Oklahoma. Before long, my older brother, Robert E. "Bob" Frampton, was born. Once again focusing on expanding their horizons, George and Cecile sold the Faxson Bank. They took little Bob up to Binger, Oklahoma, where—with the help of both grandparents—they had purchased a small bank.

It's not surprising to me that they sought to separate themselves from Faxson, where they'd experienced their great grief. Whether they consciously did that, I don't know, but I do suspect it was part of their healing process, part of keeping their little family moving forward. With the hard work that was typical of them, and their approach to banking, my parents thrived—even in those insecure days leading up to the Great Depression.

Mother occasionally spoke of those days, and one story in particular always impressed me. As things became more perilous for the country financially, rumors began to spread about how safe a person's money was in a bank. Any bank. And as those rumors took hold, almost the whole community lined up one day to make a rush on my parents' little bank. My mother was the cashier that day. She just met each customer with a smile and very slowly counted out their money until the usual closing hour of four o'clock, when she quietly closed the Teller window.

When the dust settled, they had just $100 left. They were able to replenish the cash by the next day and survived as people regained confidence. Banking definitely has its pitfalls, but my mother weathered that one calmly.

It was in 1929, with a dark cloud looming over the economy, that my parents made a move back to Lincoln, Nebraska, where a job in an established Havelock bank awaited my father. At that time, the controlling owners of the bank were the Barkley family.

On December 16th of 1929, George Frampton was made Vice President of the reorganized Farmers State Bank of College View.

The 1930's weren't easy on anyone. People had to make some really tough decisions. Farmers, for example, were faced with the choice of saving their mortgaged land, or saving the cattle they might use to start a new farm. My dad took it all to heart. During that time he worked nights and weekends to merge two struggling banks. The result is what is now Union Bank in College View.

Having a hand in starting the newly reorganized bank while still working at the Lincoln Joint Stock and Land Bank, my parents had been able to build a new Dutch Colonial house in Havelock. Oh, how my mother enjoyed that pretty house.

At that time, Havelock was a separate small town, not yet a part of Lincoln. Folks who didn't own a car, as many didn't, could get to downtown Lincoln on the interurban trolley that ran on its electric track between the two municipalities.

On October 1st of 1930, the very day that Havelock officially became a part of the City of Lincoln, I was born.

Havelock wasn't destined to be home for me for long, though. As it happened, my parents had purchased a foreclosure as a rental. Life was complicated during the austere years of the early 1930's, and to make things work out financially, my parents decided they'd put both houses on the market and then live in whichever house didn't sell.

Age two

To my mother's great dismay, her lovely Dutch Colonial sold immediately, and we moved to the former rental at 1025 South 33rd Street—a house which my mother forever remembered with little fondness.

I, on the other hand, had the run of a great neighborhood.

In those carefree days, nothing could be better than a game of 'Cowboys and Indians'. I could play that from dawn to dark. But soon the wonders of Kindergarten opened my eyes to the world. I had thought I knew it all, but the revelations I discovered in Kindergarten had me excited from Day One.

Day One was also the day of my Great Shame. My mother had walked me to Randolph Elementary on South 37th for my first day of Kindergarten. At noon, she showed up on the playground ready to walk me home. But I refused to walk with her. I was a grownup girl now. I had been to one whole half day of Kindergarten. I tossed my curls to declare my independence and walked home by myself, my mother walking a good ten paces behind trying to hide her smile.

Frampton family home on South 33rd Street in Lincoln

Those were wonderful years, highlighted by an exciting road trip eastward with my entire family to take in the 1939-1940 New York World's Fair in Queens.

1939-1940 World's Fair at night in New York.
Below, the Billy Rose Aquacade at the fair.
PHOTO BY WAELKKM

Above, 1939 Packard. Below, tired traveler.

Pictured above at age nine, I was probably wearing my favorite cowboy boots. When this photo was taken, our family was returning from the World's Fair in New York in our new 1939 Packard. I was exhausted by the time we stopped in Cleveland, Ohio, to see Dad's cousin, Eleanor Frampton. She lived a most interesting life and had a marmoset monkey as a pet.

Dad's cousin Eleanor was born in Lincoln in 1896, and arrived in Ohio in 1931 to start a dance program at the Cleveland Institute of Music. In the 1930s she was regarded as Cleveland's leading authority on modern dance. By the time she died in 1973, she had become a local institution known simply as "Frampie."

Age 9

Three

The first time I remember really sitting still, I was all of seven or eight years old. I could sit sort of still in school and church, but this time I was still as stone, on the edge of a cushiony velvet theatre seat, watching my first movie in a real movie house. When those enormous red velvet curtains rolled back and pictures began to spring onto that giant screen and music poured out from nowhere, I was enthralled. *Snow White and the Seven Dwarfs* had me in their spell. And it wasn't like you could go to a movie every Saturday. That was a treat saved up over time, and the anticipation between one movie and the next is unforgettable.

By third grade I was well into my cowboy phase. I wish I had a picture of my cowboy boots. How I enjoyed them! They had a white star on the front and I wore them every day for a full year, except for one day when I had worn a hole clear through the sole and my mother took them in for repair. It's a wonder anyone recognized me that day without my signature boots. Of course, there is no doubt in my mind that I was exceedingly dangerous playing soccer in them. I could kick the ball a country mile with those boots.

It was also around third or fourth grade that I was given another task involving money. I must have been very good at counting change by now, having had such stellar success years earlier with my soda pop sales. The school gave me the opportunity of collecting lunch money from all the children who could afford the 18¢. I'd turn in the money to the school office and ride my bike home, certain that Mother would have my own sandwich ready. I was smug thinking the cost of *my* lunch was zero.

Life was good on South 33rd. I could come and go as I pleased, unless Mother had a chore for me which could, of course, include piano practice. I'd get it done as best I could so I could go out and play. Naturally, I had learned to do the chore—or practice—correctly the first time or I would have the painful experience of being politely requested to revisit the task.

I vividly recall one particular day when my mother had given the house an extra-special cleaning because her P.E.O. chapter was coming for a meeting. When Mother hosted, the house had to be in perfect order, lace cloth on the table, silver polished to a high sheen, and every teacup inspected for chips. The best thing I could do on those days was stay out of the way. And I did.

But it was cold outside that day, so on my way out the door I hollered goodbye, grabbed a jacket, and skedaddled. A bunch of us were building a fort down on Antelope Creek that ran through our neighborhood, and I didn't want them to finish it before I got there. As I pulled the jacket on, I realized it wasn't mine. It was my brother's band jacket. Bob was eight years older than me, and already in high school. And he was pretty protective of that jacket. I knew I shouldn't be wearing it. But if I went back into the house, Mother might find something else for me to do. So I pulled it on, zipped it up, and headed for the creek.

By the time I got close enough, I could see they had a great fort going. Twice as big as I'd thought it would be, and oh, did it look grand! I tore off at a run, measured my steps, and took a flying leap across the creek. I made it too, except for one little thing. My landing foot slid in the mud on the opposite side of the creek and both my legs went out from under me. I flopped and wobbled, but the mud was just too much for me and I landed smack dab in it.

The kids had to pull me out of the muck and then they wouldn't let me play until I went home to change. They weren't about to let me get mud all over our new hideout. So I quickly took stock and reckoned I only had one choice in the matter. Generally a person has a couple of options, but not this time. It was go home and change or forget about playing. I could see it clear as a bell on their faces.

This time I didn't take a flying leap. I scurried to the little bridge, crossed it on the run, and made a bee-line to my house. My brother was going to be furious with me, and the only person who could possibly help me out of this mess was my mother. The more I worried about it the harder I ran, and it wasn't until I crashed through the back door and stopped in my muddy tracks in the middle of the kitchen floor that I remembered: Mother was hosting P.E.O.

Needless to say, neither Mother nor Brother Bob spoke to me for a good half-day.

I wasn't always the one who was in trouble back then. Not *always*. Once in a while it was my brother who got the scolding. Like the time he was just out of eighth grade and I was a first grader, and he was charged with looking after me. Which he did—along with a bunch of his friends who talked him into playing a pick-up game of kickball on a corner lot.

Naturally, being ignored by the big boys and in desperate need of diversion, I began to run around the fringes of the game, pushing myself to try and run as fast as those big guys. It didn't take long for my feet to get tangled up and I landed in the dirt, my hand cut open on a nasty piece of metal.

Now, if you think I stood there and bawled like a baby, you'd be wrong. Sort of. That would have been the last, I mean *very* last way to get help from my brother. I mean, really, have you ever seen a five-year-old who liked being called *crybaby*?

Besides, it was Bob's turn to pitch, and if I ran out there to show him my bleeding hand, the whole game would stop, and everyone would be watching me. Watching the little crybaby. So I stifled my sobs and took myself home. Another lesson in taking it on the chin, I guess.

Mother was justifiably concerned about the bloody cut as she took care of my hand. But I could see what was brewing. She had left Bob in charge of me. And not only had I sustained a fairly gruesome cut to my palm, but he had let me leave the game and walk home on my own.

Oh, yes. He was in trouble, all right. And to this day I have the scar to prove it.

I had so much freedom in those days. Within boundaries, of course. Oh, there was the bloody cut to my head when one of the kids stuck a rubber gun in my face and I reared back and clonked my head on the brick wall. And various other scrapes and bruises and hurt feelings, like any other kid. But I pretty much sailed through my childhood.

In 1941 I didn't even blink when my father told me we were moving to Des Moines, Iowa. Most likely, my eleven-year-old self saw it as a great adventure. Perhaps it was the way my parents presented it to us kids that made it so easy to accept. It meant my brother would have to change his college plans, but as I recall, it was pretty much of a lark for me. I did so love new adventures, and a new place held all sorts of tantalizing opportunities. For my dad, it was an opportunity to start a new bank for the O'Dea family. This bank was to become the Iowa State Bank.

At my new school in Des Moines, I became head of the seventh grade finance committee. When we came up with our idea for a fundraiser, the whole class wanted to participate. We had found out that when they played movies for us in the school auditorium during lunch period, someone had to change the movie reel every fifteen minutes. You had to know how to lace the film strip through the machine and start it at just the right time, just as the reel that was running came to its end.

There was nothing to it, but they would pay 2¢ per reel-change. Somehow, I convinced the school office that in light of the fact that the 7th graders were the most responsible kids in the school, and that we'd make the most perfect reel changes they'd ever seen, we got the job.

Two cents doesn't sound like much, but this was 1942, just one year after the attack on Pearl Harbor. America had jumped into World War II with both feet. Pennies weren't scarce but they weren't all that easy to come by. They were being saved in penny jars and piggy banks and cigar boxes jammed under the mattress. So we were quite thrilled to be earning all of 2¢ for the job.

One reel change a day meant we could earn up to 10¢ a week, and we all knew that a dime wasn't anything to sneeze at. In 1942 a dime could buy five popsicles. You could buy an eleven-ounce box of Kellogg's Corn Flakes for 8¢ or a loaf of bread for 9¢. And donuts were just 15¢ a dozen.

Oh yes, we had a winner of a fundraiser going on.

Looking after those pennies stuck with me for a lifetime. Just ask my children. Even they have adopted my mantra:

If you don't stop to pick up that penny,
you have too much money.

I guarantee, if you've spent much time with one of my kids, you've probably seen them stop on the sidewalk and pick up an errant penny with which someone had been careless. They learned early on to "take care of the pennies and the dollars will take care of themselves".

World War II gave us another bit of wisdom that I took to heart as well, and never forgot:

Use it up, wear it out, make it do or do without.

Those ringing words weren't just spoken, they were lived.

Like many of my friends in seventh grade, I had a keen love of sports. As it happened, my mother had a female friend who was a very fine golf instructor. That was a pretty remarkable thing in those days, so my mother jumped at the opportunity to have her teach me the game. It was a gift that has led to great times making great connections with great people.

But back to counting pennies. By the time I was a sophomore in high school I'd taken pretty good care of lots of pennies. So, my father gave me a bigger job. A couple of afternoons a week after school I'd take the bus across town to pick up deposits and other banking items from some of the bank's customers.

I wouldn't recommend trying that these days, but everything was different in those war years. With so many young men—including my brother Bob—overseas, women began to take on roles they'd not thought of before. Under the circumstances, sending a teenaged girl around Des Moines on banking business may not have been so unusual.

We surely did miss Bob. Like many college boys, he put his degree at Iowa State on hold and enlisted in the Army Air Corps. By the end of the war he'd become a Second Lieutenant, flying B-24 bombing runs over Germany and Austria. Following one of those runs they discovered their plane had 57 holes where flak had hit, but none of their crew were injured. I'll never forget the weeks following his return. Mom, Dad, and I were so proud of him and grateful for his service to our country.

As the country began to recover from World War II, Dad seized an opportunity to buy Farmer's State Bank in the little town of Davey, Nebraska. He was its President and Chairman of the Board when he purchased the controlling interest in 1948. Begun in 1903 with deposits totaling twelve thousand dollars, the bank had built a strong heritage in Davey. The little bank that had set its first cashier's salary at a mere $50 per month now had total assets of a half million dollars, which was modestly successful for a postwar smalltown bank.

Of course, buying the bank meant we were leaving Des Moines and moving back to Lincoln for my senior year in high school.

Our new home gave Dad a bit of a commute, but we did like living in the country. Our 160 acres with a farmhouse were situated on the northwest corner of Southwest 40th and West Van Dorn streets. Not long after we moved, my mother became very ill with shingles, and most of the grocery-getting and so forth fell to me.

In order to do the shopping and get back and forth to high school,

Dad got me a 1936 Plymouth 4-door. Those wide seats could hold quite a few of my friends when it was my turn to drive from Lincoln High School downtown for lunch. One time we had ten girls piled into my car and I couldn't find the gearshift—which came out of the floor in those days—for all the skirts getting in the way. But I managed and made new friends.

Remembering that old Plymouth never fails to make me smile— even when things hadn't gone so well. I'd learned to be frugal during the war years, and it stuck with me, especially that summer after my senior year when I worked part time at First National Bank in downtown Lincoln. It was my first real job in banking, filing checks.

My 50¢ per hour wage didn't add up very fast, so my thrifty self wouldn't allow me to park in the paid lots closer to the bank when I could always find a free spot six or seven blocks south of the bank on a quiet street.

One summer day after a particularly long shift I was eager to get home but found that I had a flat tire. What was I to do? I knew Mother would worry if I didn't arrive home on time.

I stewed a bit and then began to walk back to the bank, scolding my thrifty self for parking so far away from any potential help. But something stopped me. I thought, "I'll bet I can change that tire." So I turned around and walked back to my car. It couldn't be that hard, could it? Changing a tire?

Well, it wasn't all that easy, but I got the job done. Two ladies across the street watched me the whole time from their balcony. From the bits of their conversation I overheard, they'd been certain I'd never manage to get that tire changed. I'd like to have seen their faces when I tightened the last lug nut, threw the tire iron in the trunk and drove away.

I was pretty proud of myself, I must say. It might have been smarter for a teenage girl to park closer to help, but I'd never admit it.

I enjoyed that home of ours on a quarter section southwest of Lincoln. My dog and I had one hundred sixty acres to roam if we wanted to. I remember one unexpected treat that first winter. We had a particularly heavy snowfall. The drifts piled so high that I put on my skis and sailed right across the fenceposts. True story.

Senior portrait — Class of 1948
Lincoln High School

Four

By the next fall I had put away my skis and set my mind to the serious business of going to college. The University of Nebraska was good to me. And *for* me.

I do believe my Alpha Xi Delta sisters helped me navigate the many stumbling blocks a college campus can throw at a young girl. The sorority was a great place to tread softly into leadership roles, and my new sisters encouraged me to interview for campus positions. Before long I was serving on the Panhellenic Council. About the same time, I served as vice president of UNL's Women's Athletic Association. And then, of course, after my induction into Phi Chi Theta Professional Business Sorority there were even more duties and activities to manage.

It's not an easy thing to add those responsibilities to an already challenging course of study. Still, I shall always be grateful for that training ground, because when my senior year arrived, I found myself serving as president of Rho Chapter, Alpha Xi Delta. I could never have imagined then that years later my own daughter would become president of the same sorority. I was certainly more understanding of the challenges it presented Dawn than I would have been had I not shared the experience.

All in all, I remember college as an exciting, rewarding time in my life. I had a great sense of getting prepared for something. But for what?

I see now that it was during those college years, and thanks to those rewarding experiences, that I began to really lean forward into the opportunities life began to present.

Some years ago I came across a verse that has always resonated with me, both as a banking professional and as an individual. I've spoken it from memory for as long as I can remember, and never pass up an opportunity to repeat it. The verse goes like this:

> *Isn't it strange how princes and kings,*
> *and clowns that caper in sawdust rings,*
> *and common people, like you and me,*
> *are builders for eternity?*
>
> *Each is given a list of rules;*
> *a shapeless mass; a bag of tools.*
> *And each must fashion, ere life is flown,*
> *a stumbling block, or a stepping stone.*
>
> ~R. L. SHARPE

These inspired words speak volumes. I was able to walk my college path because of the stepping stones someone else had laid before me. And now I was preparing to do the same for someone coming along behind me.

It didn't come to me like a bolt of lightning, but over time I began to realize that whatever we are, whatever our background, whatever our individual capabilities and whatever the circumstances of our birth, we all have a hand in creating a path. Or fashioning a door. Or removing an obstacle. For ourselves, and for someone whose journey hasn't yet begun. The question is, will our contribution make it easier for them? Or harder? Will we create a stumbling block or a stepping stone?

In the spring of 1952, just as I was concluding my undergraduate degree, I was offered a stepping stone.

The thing about stepping stones is that you can't take all day to decide if you're going to take that step or not. I began to sense that idea in my college days. An opportunity wasn't going to sit around and wait for me to make up my mind. It could disappear as fast as it arrived while I was standing there balancing on one foot trying to decide.

I was somewhat aware of that when my friend Barb Mann began talking to me about the next step I should take after college. She was a Phi Beta Kappa, and clearly understood what it meant to have a plan.

Barb was headed back east to Tufts University. It was the best place a person interested in international law and diplomacy could go. An ambitious undertaking, to be sure. But even with her own preparations to make, she took the time to obtain admission information for a graduate business program at Radcliffe in Cambridge, Massachusetts. She did that for me. And as I greatly respected her advice, I knew I had to look into it. It's apparent that Barb understood even then the value of fashioning stepping stones.

Setting my sights on a post-graduate program in business was certainly a major step. I sensed that this prestigious Harvard/Radcliffe Program in Business Administration she told me about was an important "next step". It would greatly augment the "boots on the ground" skill set and fundamental knowledge I'd already acquired through my part-time banking experiences.

But the program was highly selective and only accepted fifty women.

If I had been born a son, Harvard might have been my next step after University. But in those years, Harvard Business School remained exclusively male. This was 1952, and it wasn't until 1959 that the first women were admitted to the MBA program at Harvard.

So with my options still limited, and with the encouragement of my dean, this daughter of a smalltown banker set herself the goal of attending the Harvard/Radcliffe program, a top business program in the country open to women. Now all I had to do was convince my father it was something I really had to do.

Whether accidentally or on purpose, I left the admission papers out on a table at home. There they were, in plain sight when a heavy snowfall kept my father from getting to work one day. Prowling around the house, he found them, and that's all it took. As he read the material outlining the program, he saw it as a perfect fit for his daughter who'd been his constant shadow since I was old enough to count the change that spilled from his pockets.

While I was weighing the pros and cons and trying to decide how to approach my father about enrolling in this prestigious program, my dad took action and seated that stepping stone in my path. Dad called me up at the university that very day and said, "Alice? I think you need to go to Harvard." And so, of course, I did. Kind of.

I went East all by myself, which actually was okay. It may surprise you to know they really kind of fussed over me. I think it may have been the fringy jacket.

I had this fringy leather jacket that I got in Yellowstone one year— the best fringy jacket of any on the University of Nebraska campus. I wore it everywhere, and naturally I took it with me back East. I loved it, so surely any new friends in Cambridge would love it, too, right?

Well, the Radcliffe girls had just never seen anything like it, but they certainly weren't going to tell me that. It would have seemed impolite.

Still, I sensed something off kilter, so I asked a new friend if there was something odd about my fringy jacket. She said, as politely as she could, "Well, it's just not something that I would have thought to bring."

What a tactful way to have said it. She spared me embarrassment while still making the point that my fringy jacket was a bit 'out of vogue.'

Somehow the newspaper managed to snap a photo of Barb Mann (standing) and I preparing to leave for our post-graduate Ivy League endeavors.

PHOTO COURTESY OF THE LINCOLN JOURNAL-STAR

I had thought that with my midwestern sophistication, armed with the best academic credentials I could muster, having experienced leadership firsthand in my collegiate days, I was prepared for the Ivy League in every way. I hadn't expected wardrobe to be a stumbling block. Aside from the fringy jacket, my sensible Pendleton wool suits seemed stuffy in that rarefied atmosphere populated by daughters of wealthy East Coast families. But my classmates were kind to me regardless. Every last one of them.

We stayed in a rooming house on Concord Avenue and we could walk to Harvard Yard and to Radcliffe. We rented horses two or three times while I was there, but we rode bicycles everywhere. Those forty-nine comrades in academia were great ladies, and I will forever be grateful to have spent time in their company. They will always be a bright and much-appreciated memory of my post-college year, a part of that first great stepping stone to my future.

My fringy jacket remained a favorite for more years than I can count. In fact, in October of 2011—sixty years and many personal and professional experiences later—I wore that fringy jacket to the state capitol when several hundred Nebraskans gathered there to lend their support to the "Occupy Wall Street" demonstrations. I just wanted to blend in and hear what they had to say, and that favorite old jacket was my perfect disguise.

Just mention that jacket and I'm sure to come up with a story or two, and they'll all circle back to Radcliffe. We were awfully lucky for those brave women who forged the path in the years before us.

It hadn't always been so 'easy' for a woman to get an education. What a blessing, then, that Radcliffe had been established seventy-five years before me as a place where intellectually-minded women could attend lectures by Harvard faculty without actually setting foot on the men's campus.

That was the dilemma, you see. Women could not be seen any-where near Harvard Yard. So, Harvard professors would come over to the Radcliffe campus and give the very same lectures they'd given the men at Harvard. By the time I arrived, the rules had relaxed enough that men from Harvard Business School could take classes on the Radcliffe campus, right alongside the women. Likewise, Radcliffe women could attend the men's seminars on the campus at Harvard, right alongside the men. But with one annoying differ-ence. The women were required to enter by the back door.

Can you imagine? I was completely nonplussed by this idea that women were not allowed to enter by way of the main door. But I was no troublemaker. I followed the rule and entered confidently through the back door as if it made no difference to me at all—as if I belonged among that collection of men who were destined to be the scions of business in the next half of the century.

I returned for an annual tea six years after having served as Panhellenic president at the University of Nebraska.

Mother and I
at the Frampton family home
outside Lincoln

Five

With a successful stint in Cambridge under my belt, I returned to Lincoln with a plan to complete my Master's Degree in Business Administration as quickly and as smoothly as possible. I worked part-time as Cashier in the Davey bank while I completed the Master's.

A Master's thesis can invoke dread in the most stellar student, and I was no different. But I waded in. My topic—Analysis of Income Sources in Small Nebraska State Banks 1946-1955—required a heavy bit of research, and most of it had to be done in the vault in the basement of the state capitol building. So day after day I walked from campus to the capitol, avoided the tiny elevator and took the stairs to the basement, and sat on the vault floor for the next few hours collecting research. You see, the information could not be removed from the vault. And there wasn't a chair in sight.

But it was a good two years, and before I managed to complete the degree and escape campus, I met Mark Dittman. From that moment on it was 'ready or not', my life was about to make a dramatic change.

I met Mark in a casual social setting, and he went out of his way to find and offer me sugar for my coffee. That impressed me, I guess, and the rest is history.

All the while, I continued to work in the Davey bank. There were just three of us—myself, my father, and the Cashier. That poor cashier just couldn't tolerate having me, a woman, and a student at that, working alongside him. It wasn't long before he threw his keys onto the desk where I was sitting and left. He never came back.

That was one of my earliest discoveries of the male ego in the workplace. Banking was such a male-dominated arena that men had not been asked to deal with a woman working alongside them— especially doing the same job they were doing. When one finds oneself in such a position, diplomacy is paramount.

Even years after that first experience, when I came back to Lincoln to assume leadership at Cornhusker Bank in 1975, I'd go to a meeting and there would be perhaps a hundred people there, only three or four of whom were women. The easy thing would have been to go and visit with the three or four women. I didn't let myself do that.

As soon as I finished the Master's in Finance and Management in 1955, Marcus Walling Dittman and I married. I remember little about the ceremony except that it was in my much-loved St. Paul United Methodist Church in downtown Lincoln. Of all the guests, I remember most clearly our mayor—Victor 'Vic' Anderson—who became governor in 1958. He and his wife Betty were to be the first to live in the newly built Governor's Mansion. And as it happened, Betty was in my P.E.O. chapter. She and the other members of the chapter were my mother's greatest supporters, so naturally they would be at my wedding. What I didn't know then was that the women of Chapter AI would be lifelong supporters of my own in years to come.

Mark was in the banking business and was given the opportunity by a group of investors to start up Central Bank in Central City, a Nebraska town of about 2,500 people with only one competitor bank. Some might be shocked to know that it never occurred to me that the top job could have been offered to me instead. Those were the times we lived in. Men led, women followed. Even so, I always sought a way to walk alongside. I never hesitated to share my opinion or make a suggestion to Mark, but I was careful not to step out in front.

It was about our fourth year of marriage when Mark and I moved westward to start the *de novo* (new) bank. Central Bank was our professional home for the next five years, where Mark was president and I was cashier.

Mark and I on opening day at Central Bank.
Our colleague Bill Peterson is on my right, and Mark is on my left.

We had a small apartment in Central City, and in 1959 Dawn Lea, our first child, was born. I couldn't know then that Dawn's many gifts would elevate her to admirable heights in the marketing and advertising arena.

Our young family was fortunate to enlist the help of Mrs. Vic Johnson as our babysitter. She and her husband, "Mr. Vic", became great friends and excellent caregivers. Mr. Vic had been a wood-worker on the "new" capitol building, and they had wonderful sto-ries to impart.

A favorite picture of mine with our firstborn, Dawn Lea, in 1960.

As young entrepreneurs, we were kind of fussed over in Central City. There was only one other bank in town, and the president's wife was in the P.E.O. chapter I transferred into. She could not have been nicer, and being welcomed into Chapter AB gave me immedi-ate connections within our new community.

My mother had gifted me two new dressy suits before we moved to Central City and did they get a workout. I had one maternity outfit, and otherwise I just made do with my usual wardrobe as I worked at the bank clear through my pregnancy. In 1959 after Dawn was born, people said they hadn't even known I was pregnant.

Two years and two months later our second child—John Framp-ton Dittman—was born. Our growing household found me still adjusting to my new roles—part-time banker, full-time mother.

In 1960, my dad had moved Farmers State Bank of Davey to Lincoln and renamed it Cornhusker Bank. In 1963, Mark was appointed president of Cornhusker Bank, even while we still lived and worked in Central City. Dad's vision for the bank put in place a stepping stone that would change the course of my life, though I didn't know it yet.

In 1964, not long after our third child, Douglas Scott, was born, Mark accepted an opportunity from a group of Missouri investors to start a new bank in Richmond. They'd been attracted by his/our suc-cess in the Central City startup, and the larger town with a popula-tion of over 5,000 was appealing to us. We found a house on the edge of town where Mark could farm "on the side". We had some farmland with a small herd of cattle, ran the bank, and watched our children flourish.

Through the 1960's, Mark and I were still officers in Dad's bank, so once every month I would lay out the children's clothes—all labeled as to what day they were to wear them—and I'd be off to Lincoln for two or three days to give some leadership to the fledg-ling Cornhusker Bank. It wasn't easy keeping the family fed and clothed and the bank details in both Richmond and Lincoln all in order, but somehow we managed.

Mark's undergraduate work had been in animal husbandry, and the farm was no mere hobby. He took it very seriously. I remem-ber one day Mark discovered we had a missing calf. It was a school holiday, so I bundled up all three kids and headed out to find the little guy. We took the station wagon as far as we could into the field, and then I took little Doug one direction and John and Dawn went another way and we were all determined to find that Charolais calf.

It took us a while, but Doug and I finally located the poor thing. It was still so weak from a challenging birth that there was no way we could walk it back to the station wagon. So I did the only thing I could. I lifted the little calf and slung it around my neck and shoulders and off Doug and I went to where we had left the car.

I soaked a scarf in a can of milk and tried to suckle the calf. It did pretty well and the kids named it Silver. They decided Silver needed to stay in the doghouse in our back yard until he got stronger. Neighbor kids would come over and ask if we'd gotten a Great Dane. "No," we'd say. "It's a calf."

Life in Richmond seemed to go along of its own accord during those years. The kids developed a great work ethic by walking beans in the summer and chopping ice in the stocktanks in the winter, and all the other chores a small farm requires.

Don't think that every chore was always done cheerfully and right on time, though. After all, they were kids. They'll tell you they heard me complain more than once that "one boy is one boy, two boys is half a boy, and three boys is no boy at all". I learned that bit of folk wisdom from my dad, and applied it to my children liberally through the years. There's a lot of joy to be heard when two or three youngsters get together, but often very little work can get done.

My mother always said she wanted her children to be equally at home in a pigpen or a parlor. Life on the Richmond farm and bank pretty much satisfied her wish for us in that regard.

One Sunday after church another mother and I decided we'd take our kids on a tour of a new local bourbon distillery. During the tour, Dawn and her girlfriend Becca Cook saw a display of postcards and a box to post them to the mail. The idea was to send one to yourself back home, or to a friend or relative. So Dawn and her friend decided to send a picture postcard of a great selection of bourbon bottles to Dawn's dad. At the bank.

Well, Richmond was a small town, and the postmaster took it upon himself to 'accidentally' misdeliver that postcard. Instead of delivering it to Mark at the First National Bank, he delivered it to our competitor, Exchange Bank.

It caused quite a ruckus in that little town as to why Mrs. Dittman was taking her children to a bourbon distillery. On Sunday.

When Dawn reached Girl Scout age, it seemed as though I had become a Girl Scout as well. And since Doug was just a little tyke and had to go wherever we went, he thought he was a Girl Scout, too. Somehow in the natural course of things I became the Girl Scout leader. I'm quite sure there are entirely too many stories associated with that time to fit into this brief memoir, so I shall resist the urge to dredge them up. I'm sure they wouldn't hold a candle to the postcard shenanigans. At least I hope not.

One particularly hectic winter I realized we needed more family time together, so I promised the kids that on Saturday I'd take them ice skating. The weather cooperated perfectly on Thursday and Friday, which was a gift, because ice skating days are scarce in Missouri.

But on Friday evening our telephone rang and the fellow on the other end of the line announced that he was with the FDIC, and the bank was to be audited. On Saturday. Ice skating day.

I thought for a moment that our outing would never happen, but then I realized there was no need for me to be there twiddling my thumbs while the FDIC fellow waded through our documents. So I put all the pertinent bank files out on our dining room table, and when he arrived I told him where to find them and that I'd left a sandwich in the fridge for him. And I took the kids ice skating.

When we got home hours later, all the files were neatly collected on the table, and the sandwich was gone. And that was that.

It's clear to me that if a person takes care of the details on a daily basis, there's no reason in the world to panic when the FDIC comes calling. It worked then, and it works now, sixty-some years later.

In my early days of banking I'd toyed with the idea of becoming an FDIC officer. Well, more than toyed. I actually checked it out. But I was a woman in a man's business, and the FDIC was more or less off limits to women in those days. It would have been nice, but now I see how it would have diverted me from accomplishing the things I'm grateful to have done as a community banker. Still, I do get a nice, prideful boost every time I mention I happen to have two grandsons who have or are working for bank regulatory agencies.

Banking business was really always on the table in those years, no matter what else was going on around us. Doug remembers playing on the floor in the dining room while his father and I chatted about the day's goings on. "What are you going to do about this builder that's having problems," I would ask, or "This family is having health problems. What could the bank do to help?" The welfare of our customers was always in the forefront of my mind.

All in all, we had life down to a somewhat manageable routine. And then Mark got an offer to head up North Hills Bank in a suburb of Kansas City. It meant another move, and somehow we took that all in stride. It was a great step up for Mark. North Hills was a much larger bank and touted the fact that the former Mayor of Kansas City was on the bank's board of directors.

We found a home at the edge of town and the kids dove into all their usual endeavors. Dawn had developed a passion for her equestrian activities and Mark enjoyed keeping a hand in farming, so we naturally gravitated to an area where keeping animals was feasible. I played tennis and golf when I could, took a less active role in banking, and kept the household together.

I was still driving to Lincoln every month and somehow managed to survive several years as president of the Winding River Girl Scout Council. Let me tell you, that was a full-time position. Unpaid, of course.

Under Mark's leadership, North Hills Bank's assets grew well, and life eventually settled into an ever-changing yet familiar routine.

Our children were the apple of his eye, though they all remember that he was quite demanding of them. Dawn recalls in particular one time when she came in third place in a horse show. His reaction left no doubt in her mind as to his expectation.

"You're not going to do that again," he said. "Only first or second place will do." He expected so much of all three of our children, but his love was unconditionally felt by them.

And then Mark became ill with not one but two kinds of cancer.

Christmas 1967 - John, Dawn, Doug, myself and Mark

Marcus Walling Dittman

Six

There's an unsettling, scrambled order to things when a family member is brought low by cancer. In the 1970's there weren't many options for battling the disease, and so it took its course. Though he met with multiple specialists and at last went to the Mayo Clinic in Rochester, the prognosis was the same. Mark had two kinds of cancer, and it just wasn't possible to survive both.

When Mark died on April 24, 1975, I found myself in a Kansas City suburb with three children to usher through their grief and a need to sketch out some kind of future for us. I could have stayed put and held down a teller job in a downtown bank. That might have felt like a safe thing to do. But a small Nebraska bank like my father's that had now grown to nearly $8 million in assets posed a greater opportunity than anything I would find in Kansas City.

Dawn was fifteen, John was thirteen, and Doug was eleven when their father died. They were quite involved with their school, sports, and friends. But I found myself looking to Lincoln. I'd been active in my father and mother's bank throughout my marriage, and Mark had been an officer in Dad's bank, as well. Now my dad was ready to retire, so it was a fairly obvious decision to return to Lincoln and step into his shoes.

Doing that was easier said than done. There was an incredible puzzle of business dealings to sort out with Mark's bank, and nearly as many puzzles on the personal side. Mark had been very ill for three years, and there was a great deal to manage, debts to clear, and obligations to settle. I didn't think about it being hard. I just did it. I took things one step at a time, and then had a little powwow with the children about what we should do. I managed to achieve consensus that we should head north. In a mere ninety days I tied up the business dealings, sold the house and the cattle, packed the horse trailer, and moved my little family to Lincoln.

We put everything we wanted to take with us into that old trailer—minus the horse—and left Kansas City. I had my three kids, plus one of their friends who came along for moral support, a crying cat, and a horse trailer that would high center the car if you approached a railroad track wrong. But we were moving toward our destination until, about an hour after dark, we ran out of gas in the middle of nowhere.

All five of us, minus the yowling cat, walked to the nearest farmhouse and were lucky they had a fuel tank. They loaded a couple of gas cans and my three-plus-one kids into the back of their truck and in less than an hour we were back on the road. What would I have done if that generous farmer hadn't been home?

That trip was the kind of experience I'd wish to forget if it hadn't been such an important stepping stone to the rest of my life. It was July of 1975. I was forty-four years old and finally stepping back onto my career path. I had just been made president of Cornhusker Bank—the first woman president of any commercial bank in Lincoln or Omaha. Though I didn't sense it at the time, it would be the first of many firsts to come.

I'd always said, "No one can out-small me."

I had learned to reconcile a small bank's daily business with nothing but a pencil, paper, and a reliable adding machine. Come to think of it, that adding machine didn't even require electricity. I can still feel how its worn handle fit into my palm. And the sound of its clacking keys will most likely ring in my ears through eternity.

The greater point, though, is the fact that working with my father and mother in the smallest of small banks with only three employees gave me a firsthand view of how a healthy bank should interact with its community—how a banker is responsible to not make loans that keep people mired in unreasonable debt.

I've always believed that debt is like fire. It can warm you or burn you. One of the greatest gifts a bank can bestow is to help a person grow their way out of debt. Another is not to burn a customer with debt he or she has no hope of repaying.

When you enter into an agreement, it has to be fair on both sides of the desk. I learned early how to deal gently with customers who hadn't fully thought things through, like the 55-year-old woman who came to me wanting a loan to get a second college degree—on top of the debt she still had from her first loan. I showed her that at her age she'd have little hope of getting through college and working long enough to pay off both loans before she retired. Her dream was exciting and laudable, but it was not realistic and would cause her more financial stress in her retirement years.

It's true that I have always said at Cornhusker Bank we finance people's dreams. But that doesn't always mean loaning a person a lofty sum. Sometimes it simply means knowing when to honor an overdraft. Something like that can save a person's reputation, and that's important.

Dad always said that a banker is the only damn fool who brags about his debts. He meant that every deposit a customer makes is a debt the bank owes *back* to them—one hundred cents on the dollar. The more deposits a bank takes in, the greater its assets, and the greater its debt to its customers.

It's critical for a banker to realize that those customers are trusting him or her with their deposits. That's a lesson that some bankers may have forgotten, and it can lead to some really bad consequences for the bank.

This was the mindset I carried with me into those first days as a single mother. It didn't take long to settle our new household, get the kids enrolled in school, and start working full-time at the bank.

That first night after the first full day of work I came home exhausted. I begged the kids to give me ten minutes to lie down and then I'd take them out for supper. Later, when I paid for our meal, I realized our supper at the Hiway Diner had cost just slightly less than I'd made that day. My salary as president of the bank that first year averaged out to just over $7 an hour.

It's impossible to note how often I breathed a prayer of thanks for the stepping stones my parents laid in my path…stepping stones that led me toward a future that would sustain my family. Stepping stones that put me in a position to use the skills I'd honed in a business I'd come to love.

Back in December of 1959, as Mark and I were developing the bank in Central City, my father had moved the Farmer's State Bank of Davey to Lincoln. Quite by chance, I had read an article explaining the value of old German war bonds. That article triggered my memory of some bonds I'd seen tucked away on a corner shelf in the bank's vault. Sale of those bonds brought in the modest sum of $4,000. In those days, that amount was nearly equivalent to the bank's annual profit, and it funded the move to 2834 North 14th Street. The relocated bank was launched with modest ceremony under its new name:

CORNHUSKER BANK

The new bank's small board of directors included my dad George, my mother Cecile, my brother Bob, and me. I had been made Vice President of New Accounts. The assets held by the bank on the day of the move amounted to $695,000. Between December of 1959 and December of 1960, the bank's assets grew to $1.03 million.

Dad's decision to move the bank to Lincoln proved to be a good one, and as it was one of only two city-county banks north of the Burlington railroad tracks, Dad's choice of location was well positioned for growth.

In 1963, when Mark was elected president of Cornhusker Bank, we were still heading up the bank in Central City. By 1964, Cornhusker Bank's earnings had grown by 22%. Four years after the move assets had doubled from $1.03 million in 1960 to just over $2 million in 1964. The board of directors grew as well, and now included we four Framptons, my husband Mark, Forrest Hutson, Leicester Hyde, John Stewart, Karl Witt, Robert McGill, and Norman Bulling. Dad was chairman and Mark was president. Mother and I were vice presidents. And yes, with Dawn and John born in 1959 and 1961, just two years and two months apart, I well remember the daily challenges two banks and two babies presented.

During the years after Mark and I relocated to Richmond, Missouri in 1964 and subsequently to Kansas City in 1972, our work with Cornhusker Bank remained a high priority. My monthly trips to Lincoln kept me comfortably involved in the bank's inner workings. Some of my efforts were centered upon my role as Vice President of New Accounts, and some involved the more delicate intricacies of navigating human resources.

A bank's physical surroundings form important first impressions in the minds of a bank's customers. I was constantly aware that our premises should be tasteful and carefully kept, including the parking lots. Employees learned by my father's example, and then mine, that a part of their job was to make sure no litter marred a customer's experience, either inside or outside. If I could shovel snow away from the entrance on a Sunday morning after church, they wouldn't mind picking up a bit of litter now and then. It seemed the most natural thing to do, so I was surprised when the Lincoln Journal-Star took note of it:

> There's a story in the woman who believes she shouldn't ask anyone else to do anything she wouldn't do herself. So if the drive-through tubes at the bank get clogged, it just might be Dittman unclogging them. If the parking lot needs sweeping, she'll do it.
> -LINCOLN JOURNAL-STAR

I always felt that the same attention to detail was necessary with regard to the bank's employees as well—in their choices of clothing, hairstyles, shoes, and the like. Everything served to make a statement not just about them, but about the bank itself. It wouldn't do to have customers think that if we were careless with our property or personal appearance, we might also be careless with their money.

Wardrobe isn't always the easiest thing to manage, especially for an employee who might be managing a house full of children in addition to working full time at the bank. My awareness of this multi-faceted dilemma resulted in two essential policies which had very positive effects for Cornhusker Bank.

The first change came about as the result of a see-through blouse. I will give the employee who wore it the benefit of the doubt that the flurry of getting a household dressed and off to school might not always leave time for a quick mirror check of oneself on the way out the door. I certainly did understand how the hectic routine of marshaling children and backpacks and breakfast might have conspired to leave attention to her own wardrobe pretty low on the totem pole.

Regardless of how attractive the woman's blouse was, it was simply not appropriate for the business environment. And it was my job to tell her so…in the kindest way possible.

But that got me thinking about what we as an employer could do to help alleviate that problem for all our staff. The solution was uniforms, or what I referred to as "career dressing".

By working with a design company who dealt with uniforms for flight attendants and the like, we developed a line of clothing our employees could choose from. The jackets, skirts, blouses, ties, and so on were interchangeable. Three days each week employees would wear their choice of pieces, and the other two days they could dress in their own personal wardrobe.

THE LINCOLN STAR
Friday, December 23, 1988
PAGE 10

Lifescape

Uniform career dressing catching on in work place

By Gerry Switzer
Of The Lincoln Star

Customers do a double take when they suddenly realize there's a like thread woven into the wearing apparel of Cornhusker Bank employees.

But by combining different pieces of the wardrobe each employee maintains an individualized look.

"It's really fun where we go to lunch," said Cheryl Socha, teller supervisor at the bank at 10th and Cornhusker.

"A group of us walk in somewhere and people look and then they look again."

Some inquire whether the bank employees are a vocal group ready to perform or members of a flight crew staying over in Lincoln.

Uniform career dressing is becoming fashionable.

Employees say they like it because the decision about what to wear most mornings is made for them.

And employers like it because they know their staff will show up dressed to project a professional image.

COMMUNITY BANK implemented career dressing for employees about 18 years ago. Because of the variety available in mix-and-match coordinate outfits, staff members are uniformly dressed but not identically attired.

Some combination of this year's uniform is required on Mondays and Fridays and optional on Wednesdays.

"Mondays and Thursdays, staff may wear what they choose. But it's usually last year's uniform, they say. And on free choice days, some combine pieces from this year's outfit with those from last year or the year before.

This year's uniform options for women consist of a camp shirt with navy and one paisley print with navy, teal and camel tones — in a choice of several styles, two blouses — one solid teal color and one paisley to match the paisley skirt, a navy jacket available in a variety of styles and lengths, navy slacks, a paisley scarf, and a braided belt of the paisley fabric.

For men, this year's uniform is a navy blazer and coordinated slacks, and a tie which generally either matches or picks up a color in the women's uniform.

FOR EXAMPLE, here was a sampling of the uniform dress of three bank employees on a Friday when this reporter visited the bank:

— Becky Polivka, a teller, was wearing a paisley skirt and matching scarf draped over the shoulder of a solid teal blouse which picked up the teal shade in the predominantly blue and teal paisley skirt.

— Socha was wearing the same paisley skirt with a matching paisley blouse to form a two-

piece dress. She accented the outfit with a tie at the neck and a braided belt at the waist.

— Sally Jacobs, new accounts officer, was wearing the plain teal-colored blouse with a navy skirt and matching longer-style jacket.

— Bank President Alice Dittman was wearing the navy suit with a shorter jacket and the paisley scarf.

Dittman said she started the career dressing at Cornhusker Bank to encourage people to dress in a professional manner and to enable some staff members who couldn't afford to purchase business clothing to dress professionally. This also eliminated employee dressing competition, she said.

Rarely has she encountered any protest from employees because they are told about the uniform dressing when they are hired, Dittman said. Everyone is required to wear the uniform including part-time people. However, no one is required to buy the entire mix-and-match outfit.

The bank pays for half, up to $190, of what an employee orders. According to Jacobs, employees are not required to buy the entire outfit, but most full-time women employees do to allow for variety in mixing and matching.

If they purchased the entire outfit this year consisting of two skirts, two blouses, a jacket, a pair of slacks, a belt and scarf, the total cost was $381, of which the bank paid $190 and the employee paid the remaining $191.

If they purchased the minimum required pieces, the total cost was $162 with the bank paying half of that amount. Part-time people are required only to purchase a skirt or slacks and one blouse.

CUSTOMERS seem to like the uniforms.

"These really look sharp," said customer De-

lores Ulrich. "I always look to see if they all have them on."

And 25-year Cornhusker customer Jack Curran said, "I just love them. They look dignified and give the bank a good image."

Commercial Federal Savings and Loan Association also gets "tremendous comments from customers" on its uniform dress for customer-contact employees, said Dick Fitzgerald, first vice president and regional manager.

He said Commercial Federal had a uniform dress policy in the late 1960s and early 1970s, but because of the protests during the "liberal period," the policy was dropped.

But four years ago, the Omaha-based savings and loan association revitalized the program and employees have been receptive to the professional image they have established as well as the money they save by not having to buy all their career clothes themselves.

The company pays for a portion of the total four-suit wardrobe employees purchase every two years.

But unlike the Cornhusker Bank plan, the Commercial Federal uniform consists of identical suits, all of the same style skirt or pants and jacket. The employee may choose blouses or skirts as long as they conform to the standard set by Commercial Federal — what color outfit colors and have a collar with ties may be worn.

"Employees make an individual statement in the ties they wear" with the suits, Fitzgerald said.

AMONG OTHER businesses in Lincoln that have gone to uniform dressing are health providers and health services offices.

For example, the all-female staff at the office of Lincoln dentist Robert Glenn went to uniform styles of slacks and tops about three years ago, according to Barb Ketterer, scheduling coordinator.

Each employee is given a clothing allowance for the uniform outfits, she said.

While financial institutions traditionally have been the prime industry in which office staff are uniformly dressed, health services are becoming the number two area.

John Livingston, president of Prestige Fashions of Marlin, Texas, said career dressing is becoming a trend nationwide. His firm, which supplied Cornhusker Bank with its uniforms, has grown from six to 250 employees in 11 years.

"On Mondays people in their current outfit that helps both the employee and employer, he said.

"Someplace in an organization is a woman with three children and no husband" who needs this extra fringe benefit, he said.

It also is a fringe benefit for the employer because it assures that the staff at all times will be professionally attired.

He said career people want uniforms in the same styling and fabrics they would buy at better local stores. Fabrics must be good quality to withstand frequent wearings, and career dressing can't include faddish items.

SINCE CAREER dressing may involve people of varying heights and sizes, Livingston's company sends a representative to measure each of the employees of a customer firm so the uniforms are custom fit, he said.

When financial institutions in Texas and across the country began having some financial problems, Prestige Fashions made a push into the health services market.

This is a growing market, said Livingston, who believes more and more businesses will see the value of career dressing as the only fringe benefit in which both the employee and employer benefit.

Wearing mix-and-match outfits are Cornhusker employees Cheryl Socha (left), Brian Johnson, Becky Polivka, Sally Jacobs.

As it turned out, our employees appreciated it. Having the uniforms, which were in reality attractive business suits and ensembles, removed a small stress while at the same time making the subtle suggestion that we all were part of the same team.

The second change, which I believe is still implemented today, was job-sharing. This practice allowed two people to fill a full-time position, with one working morning hours and the other working the afternoon portion.

Mothers who wished to work away from home but needed to be available to pick up children after school, for example, found the job search quite frustrating. Much of the work advertised as part time did not pay on a professional scale. Job duties were often menial and below the skill level of the women looking for work. We addressed that with our job-sharing program. We made it possible for two women to share one professional position, utilizing skills they'd often acquired through a college education and allowing them to experience the job satisfaction of which they were deserving though working part time.

Job-sharing was a boon to our staffing needs at Cornhusker Bank and at the same time gave us a bit of pride that we were serving an often overlooked segment of our community. And we needed the staff, because Cornhusker Bank was growing.

Creative use of our staff and our space has served Cornhusker Bank well. Even the newspaper took note when my dad planted a corn patch at the edge of the parking lot on North 14th Street in 1966. The photo caption read:

Frampton is tall, but his corn patch a few paces away
from his bank building is taller.

Dawn, Doug, Alice and John

$\mathcal{S}$even

Prior to moving my family to Lincoln in 1975, Cornhusker Bank's assets had surpassed the $4 million mark. In 1971 we had added our first separate drive-up branch at Belmont Plaza Shopping Center on the northwest side of 11th and Cornhusker Highway. It did so well that later we requested permission to open a second drive-up bank at 1300 North 27th Street, which opened in February of 1974.

I say "we requested permission" because a bank can't just decide to open a new branch or an additional drive-up location and put up an "open for business" sign. These things are regulated by the federal government, to ensure that a community doesn't constantly face the prospect of too much competition causing smaller banks to fail or spend too much money on facilities and put the bank at risk.

Regulation is what one might think of as a necessary evil. No matter how clearly a bank's directors might see the need for a new branch, the regulating board will look at the numbers and decide yay or nay. It's a necessary thorn in the side of every banker, and a frequent topic of conversation. Over the years I was occasionally quoted issuing my own opinions on the matter. I remember one article in particular that appeared in an issue of the American Banker's Association Journal:

...If there was a common theme to the ABA town meetings this spring, it was that bankers are restless; they're fed up with overregulation and they're angry. As Alice Dittman, president of the Nebraska Bankers Association, put it, "We've got 26% of the market share and 90% of the regulation."

...Banking's market share may be down, but our blood pressure's rising. Bankers are talking treason these days. It's a good sign.

~HEALTHY TREASON; BRANDON, WILLIAM H., JR.,
ABA BANKING JOURNAL

I wouldn't go so far as to describe myself as "angry" much less "treasonous", but perhaps this article does reveal the frustration many bankers feel when a new bit of regulation appears. In spite of it all, Cornhusker Bank weathered the regulation storms and grew in size and stature. As we did so, we were able to add more financial services, like making individual loans up to $100,000. As a result of the steady growth, in June of 1975, just as I was about to step into the presidency, Cornhusker Bank's assets had reached $8 million. In the next twenty-one years of my tenure, those assets would grow to over $140 million—a growth of over $6 million per year.

The bank wasn't the only thing exploding in those days. My children were growing like weeds. Dawn was graduating high school by now and I was becoming accustomed to the idea of having a college co-ed in the family. Just to keep us from becoming too awfully serious, my youngest (who would have been about fourteen at the time) managed to inject humor on a fairly regular basis. Sometimes he planned it, sometimes it just happened.

One Saturday morning we were all in the kitchen, as was fairly typical in our house. In my early days as president of the bank I had struck a deal with my two colleagues—Ken Ward and Jim Mastera—that I would get Saturday mornings off. It worked out comfortably for us all.

That particular Saturday morning I had just boiled some eggs to make potato salad. As I removed one of the eggs from the kettle, Doug, ever the inquisitive child, wondered aloud what might happen if we cooked an egg in the microwave oven.

"Don't even think about it," I warned.

And then I found myself thinking, "I wonder what *would* happen?" So I gave him the nod.

When the microwave beeped, Doug removed the egg and tapped it, but nothing happened. I said, "Try it again." He tapped the egg and again, nothing happened.

"Well," I said, "I guess nothing's going to happen."

But Doug persisted. He went over to the sink, tapped the egg a third time, and it exploded all over the ceiling. There were little yellow granules everywhere. It was really amazing how that happened. The adventure that followed was figuring out how to get all the egg yolk off of the popcorn ceiling. And yes, the kids did help clean it up. Doug had a blister on one finger. I felt badly about that, since I was the one who suggested he should go ahead and tap that hot egg.

Armed with three degrees and twenty years of banking experience, I had felt ready to assume the mantle of presidency. Yet, sensing the need for an immersion course in banking to refine and retool, I wasted no time reserving a spot at the Wisconsin School of Banking. I felt certain it was exactly what I needed to widen my focus. The WSB was a place where I could completely shut out the world and concentrate on both new and traditional banking practices I may have known about but hadn't had time to see them in relation to our bank's culture.

Beginning in 1978, for the next three summers I would attend a resident WSB session in Madison, Wisconsin. In the intervening months I would research and write papers on prescribed subjects. The exercise was invaluable in keeping my mind attuned to the larger world of finance.

I certainly did welcome the invigorating challenge, although welcoming my assigned roommate that first summer was another matter entirely. The day I arrived for the two-week class, I checked in and found the room that had been assigned to me. A rather mannish sport coat lay on one of the beds, so I laid claim to the other bed. It never occurred to me the coat actually belonged to a man!

When the coat's owner showed up at my door we were both in for a shock. He was assigned to be my roommate.

Well, we had a good chuckle out of how he had rationalized the fact that his roommate's name was 'Alice' and I had rationalized the presence of the sport coat. After a congenial moment, we backtracked to the registration desk and got things straightened out. My registration listed my title as bank president, and evidently the registrar hadn't considered the possibility that a bank president might actually be a female.

That immersion course was worth its weight in gold in preparing me for this next phase of my career. With more degrees than most bankers, I had confidence that I could hold my own.

It was a rather fractured time, though. I must admit there were occasions when my talents did not quite rise to the pinnacle of perfection. At dinnertime, for example, when my youngest son was prone to evaluate my culinary efforts. One night when I had dashed home to put food on the table before I had to dash on to a business dinner, Doug quipped, "Not bad, Mom. Only two out of three burned."

That really stung, because the third thing—the only thing I hadn't burned—was the lettuce.

✽

Nobody undertakes a bank presidency without the kind of support one can rely upon one hundred percent. For me there were many such individuals whose skill and loyalty meant everything to me. My first line of support always came from executive vice presidents Ken Ward and Jim Mastera, and later on Steve Lindgren. We made a good team. If any two of us thought a new idea was the way to go, the third one went along. And sometimes I was the third one. We had a great working relationship which is so important. It's such a gift when you love to go to work, when work is not a burden. When those you work alongside are skilled at navigating the stepping stones and stumbling blocks.

Occasionally these teammates were the very ones who laid challenges directly at my feet. One such challenge resulted in my entry into the speaking circuit in Lincoln.

One morning as I arrived at the bank, Ken approached me with a date I should add to my calendar. He had accepted, on my behalf, a speaking engagement for a business luncheon just two days hence. By that time in my career I'd spoken at dozens of events, but never as the leader of a bank, and seldom to a gathering of over a hundred businesspeople who were potential customers. I admit I quaked for an instant and immediately urged Ken to give the speech, as he normally would have if my father hadn't been available. He adamantly refused. It was paramount, he said, that I establish my presence in the community as the bank's president. We were, after all, a community bank. These were the people we served.

I had to admit Ken was right, and I imagine my children ate take-out for the next two evenings as I feverishly prepared my speech. I haven't a clue what I said, but I do remember forcing myself to bound up the steps to the podium as if I just couldn't wait to speak. It was important, I realized, to show an energetic, enthusiastic approach. If I walked as if I dreaded the moment, the audience might dread hearing what I had to say. Throughout the rest of my career I reminded myself to maintain that energetic approach to public speaking.

✻

I had recognized early on the advantage we had as a community bank. Larger banking institutions had hierarchies of approval that had to be scaled before a change could be instituted. But at Cornhusker Bank, we could make a decision at 9:00 a.m. and begin implementing it by 10:00 a.m. That was a part of our corporate persona that helped us remain strong amid the competition.

Our open-mindedness resulted in community projects, too, which I was proud to be a part of. Our bank was instrumental in moving an historic bank building to a turn-of-the-century Main Street on Nebraska's fairgrounds. We also helped develop a new banking exhibit at the Lincoln Children's Museum. We launched an annual "One Day Without Shoes" project to collect shoes for the People's City Mission, never imagining that eight years later the project would have collected over one hundred sixty thousand pairs of shoes for Lincoln's homeless.

The Day Without Shoes venture isn't just Cornhusker Bank reaching out to the community, though. It's the bank facilitating a project that involves more than a hundred local organizations reaching the community in their own unique ways to magnify the effectiveness of what otherwise would have been a much smaller accomplishment. Those organizations do the work of encouraging members to donate, and picking up the full bins to deliver them to the bank. High schoolers come in and tie up the shoes so they stay in pairs, and sort them by size and so on. It makes me feel good to see so many people working together on such a worthy project. That kind of thing might not happen in lots of places in this country, but it's no surprise to anyone that it happens frequently here in Lincoln, Nebraska.

Many Lincolnites know family names like the Woods Brothers. The name stretches clear back to 1873 starting with Col. Frederick Woods and his three sons, Mark, Frank, and George. We know them as a major force in Nebraska real estate. But there's a rather astounding list of other ventures in which the Woods family played a major part: nurseries, river construction, farming, telephone companies, street car companies, truck manufacturing, even aviation. Theirs is a legacy from which Lincoln prospered.

Another is the Seacrest family. Like the Woods family, the Seacrest philanthropic mind set seems to roll from generation to generation like well-placed dominoes, gaining strength as the decades pass.

Each year new family names crop up, making their first strides toward a legacy that will keep Lincoln maintaining its reputation as one of our country's desirable places to live.

I was always so grateful to other community leaders who were willing to come alongside me from time to time. Or for that matter, who let *me* come alongside *them*. I'd have an idea I knew the bank would support, but it might not be something the bank could undertake singlehandedly. I'd look for a natural fit, approach that business or individual with the idea, and a large percentage of the time they'd come right on board.

A good example is Ross Hecht, who collaborated with us to build a 28-unit apartment building for low-income elderly. Together we built something that we all could be proud of, something the community needed.

Some years ago when it was still vital to keep a phone book on my desk, I paused out of curiosity to check the yellow pages. Even I was surprised to find twenty-two pages of organizations and groups advertising their services to help people in need. But this is Lincoln, and that's what we've always done here.

These are the kinds of things that give our Cornhusker Bank employees pride—giving back to a community that exercises its servant's heart.

Altruistic gestures aren't confined to corporations and nonprofits, though. Sometimes a gem of an idea occurs to an individual, and once the idea falls on the right ears, it just might take flight.

That very phenomenon happened when Lincoln artist Anne Burkholder first imagined a local building with gallery showrooms, studios where artists could produce their art, and apartments where the artists could live close to their work.

I happened to be in her home one of the first times Anne

mentioned what she called her "pipe dream" in conversation. What if she could sell her large home and much of its furnishings and use the proceeds to purchase a building—perhaps in the Haymarket—and live there herself while she developed her dream galleria? She laughed at the idea, but I could see it was something she'd thought deeply about.

I'll never forget stepping out of her home and turning to say goodbye. As she stood waving, I was immeasurably struck by the magnitude of Anne's dream. She would give up that beautiful home for an apartment in an old building, all to make a place where artists like herself could live and create. What a generous idea it was.

Not long after, I was leaving lunch in the Haymarket with a colleague when I saw a rather run-down building just around the turn southeast of Lincoln Station. It was just the kind of thing Anne had described. At my earliest opportunity I phoned Anne and told her I'd pick her up. I had something I wanted her to see.

And that was that. Her artist's mind took that old building and turned it into an artist's paradise. She and the artists who have made it their home have flourished within those walls, and watched the product of their hands and hearts go out the door in the hands of not just Lincolnites or Nebraskans, but art lovers from all over the country. Now the Burkholder Project has 36 art and design studios, loft apartments, and three levels of galleries, featuring artists of all disciplines and styles.

It's a dream fulfilled.

I've said many times that *at Cornhusker Bank we finance dreams*. It might sound like a nice slogan, but when you're a part of it, it's the most gratifying experience a person can have. I do love figuring out how to make a loan work for the customer and the bank. It's my very own art form, a special way in which I, too, can be creative.

There were unintended consequences to allowing myself some creativity. It brought interesting projects to the attention of city leadership and resulted in a Kiwanis award for Distinguished Service. At the time, I became one of only four women who had received that honor in the previous eighty years.

✳

The 1980's proved to be a powerful decade of growth for my family, for Cornhusker Bank, and for me. I began to hold positions on boards, often rising to positions of leadership. As it happened, not only was I the first female bank president in Lincoln, but by 1993 I was the first woman to have led the Nebraska Bankers Association, the Lincoln Chamber of Commerce, the Nebraska Chamber of Commerce and Industry, and the Community Bankers Council, which is part of the American Bankers Association.

To do all of that, and do it well, I had to step out of my comfort zone. There's a good bit of weighty business to be taken care of when you're at the helm, but there was fun, too. It had become tradition that when the Nebraska Bankers Association met, we'd have a golf outing. So the year I was president, I held the event at the Country Club of Lincoln where I often golfed. As was our habit, the NBA president would tee off first to get things rolling. So after lunch, I headed out to the tee box to do the honors, and was stopped by one of the club's staff members.

"You can't play yet, Mrs. Dittman. It's not one o'clock."

In the early 1990's, that club still reserved the prime morning hours for men golfers only. Women could not be on the course until after one o'clock. But I was Nebraska Bankers president, and the president had the duty of teeing off first. I calmly explained the situation, but it made no difference to the employee. So with a smile I just walked on past, tee'd up my ball, and got things rolling. Nobody else had challenged my right to do so. And why would they? I was the host of the event, after all.

I never let those things affect me. If I'd stayed in my comfort zone, I might have nominated some fellow to do the honors for me that day. But I certainly had not built a career in an historically male work arena only to become invisible when it came time to play. I intended to continue moving bit by bit through experiences where women were customarily ignored, and simply do the work and make my presence quietly known.

I feel compelled to add it was in 1993 that I became the first woman to sit on the board of the Country Club of Lincoln.

John and I at our 11th & Cornhusker
bank headquarters

Eight

When we moved into our new headquarters at 11th and Cornhusker Highway in 1979, it felt to me as if we put the final jewel in
Cornhusker Bank's crown. I remember the construction process as
an exhilarating time. We were very intentional in the design, making
certain the two-story brick building would meet the needs of both
staff and customers and give a pleasing aspect to the surrounding
area.

I was always particularly satisfied with the way the second floor
balcony worked out. In our small initial buildings, our employees
had been easily accessible to one another. You couldn't go ten minutes without greeting a co-worker, or easily finding them in order
to conduct a bit of business. I worried that if we built a three-story
building, much of that camaraderie and accessibility would be lost,
and that it might feel isolating to some.

The dilemma was happily resolved when we decided to put an
atrium in the middle of the second floor. Now anyone walking from
one office to another would be in view not only of those on the second floor, but those on the first level, as well. Our growing staff was
pleased with the outcome, and years later—in February of 2017, to

be exact—when we built an even larger main office at 84th and O Streets, we repeated the atrium, although much larger in size. The new main bank, I should add, would have the same square footage as the White House.

I must say it was a high compliment when Nebraska businessman and friend Duane Acklie asked permission to emulate the 11th and Cornhusker design in a bank he was building in Norfolk. I recall him telling me that our new main bank gave the perception that Cornhusker Bank was the third largest bank in Lincoln. Of course I gave the appropriate permissions, and savored the compliment.

In those years, our wonderful new building on 11th and Cornhusker seemed as large as we would ever require. Everyone was eager for the day we would cut the ribbon and declare the new headquarters open for business. But the day before the grand opening, a problem of some sort held up the landscaping crew. Pallets of sod were ready to install, but unless the workers could somehow pick up the pace, the grounds just weren't going to be ready in time for the opening ceremony. Anyone who has ever laid sod knows just what a brutal task it is. Picking up the pace is an impossibility. What they needed was more help.

This time it was my children who came to the rescue. They pitched in and helped lay the final rolls of sod and finished hosing down the sidewalks just as the sun was setting.

It was no surprise to my children that they'd be drafted for the task. They'd often seen their mother with a broom sweeping the entrance in the morning, or patrolling the parking lot for litter. It was the kind of thing their grandfather would have done, too. In fact, my father gave a great smile when I told him how his grandchildren had risen to the occasion and saved the day.

✤

Beginning in the 1980's I had often found myself traveling outside Nebraska on business. In October of 1981, not long after I landed in San Francisco for a major convention of the American Bankers Association, an article appeared in the *San Francisco Chronicle*. It came about during a time of increased regulation and the rise of larger banks swallowing up the smaller community banks.

The popular writer of a weekly news column did his research and had come to the conclusion that community banks were about to disappear. According to Donald K. White, that was a good thing. An expected thing. And he did not pull any punches in his weekly article.

Small Bankers' Last Hurrah
Donald K. White — Banquet Circuit column
San Francisco Chronicle
Friday October 2, 1981

The bankers are coming! The bankers are coming! Stand by San Francisco.

Don't try to get into Trader Vic's for the next five days. It is booked cheek-by-jowl by delegates to the American Bankers Association's annual convention.

A private room at Ernie's restaurant is out of the question. Ernie's has been booked by Citibank, Bankers Trust and Bank of America for the last 18 months. The Blue Fox's private rooms are fully reserved.

Tomorrow Bank of America will take over the Carnelian Room starting at 11 a.m. for a simple brunch of 2,000 delegates. The next day Chase Manhattan Bank will take over the Carnelian's main dining room at 11 a.m. to entice bankers it wants to impress with an eggs benedict brunch for 500.

Chase Manhattan and New York's Irving Trust favor Peking Duck dinners as a way of impressing their peers.

Both banks have lined up elaborate, nine-course duck dinners in private rooms at Kan's restaurant.

Private clubs—Pacific Union, Bohemian, Burlingame Country, no others need apply—have been booked for bankers' parties.

If the weather stays warm, Saks, I. Magnin and the boutiques along Post and Union streets will do booming business. The bankers and their spouses have been told to wear woolies to San Francisco. If the annual heat wave hits they'll rush out to do a clothing retrofit.

What San Francisco's hotels, restaurants, cabbies, bartenders and merchants will be witnessing is the last gasp of the commercial banking business in the United States as we have known it since the early 1930s.

There are 14,500 commercial banks in this country, which is about 14,000 more than any sophisticated economy needs.

Is there really a need for the Cornhusker Bank of Lincoln, Neb., in the grand scheme of things? Alice M. Dittman, the bank's president, will claim there is.

Or for the Walnut Valley State Bank of El Dorado, Kan.? Its board chairman, Clifford Stone, here for the convention, is sure to say that his bank fits a special community need that no big banks can fill.

The fact is that the American banking system is going through rapid changes as a result of deregulation.

Old-fashioned "mom and pop" banks protected by state laws that prohibit branch banking, can no longer survive in the face of competition from big banks, nationwide brokerage houses, large savings and loan associations, insurance companies and money market funds.

By the time the American Bankers Association convenes again in San Francisco five years from now, the commercial banking business will have gone through a complete metamorphosis.

Safe to say there will be far fewer than 14,500 banks represented.

Nationwide banking, as practiced in every other

industrialized nation, has been too long forbidden by law in the United States.

A fragmented banking system is anachronism in these days of electronic banking. When you can transfer funds electronically to any corner of the world is there a need for parochial bankers?

The "mom and pop" corner store bank will say there is, but they have yet to feel the heat of real competition.

For them, the San Francisco convention may be their last hurrah. ¤

Last hurrah, my foot. But that was the prevailing notion among folks who didn't realize the tenacity and ingenuity of the smaller banks. My father had safely steered a course through the worst years in banking history at that point, and the principles he put in place were a constant source of strength and security for Cornhusker Bank. The support I was seeing from our community continued to convince me that a "neighborhood bank" was exactly what our "sophisticated economy" in Lincoln needed. 14,000 too many banks? I think not.

And neither did my father. But in the weeks following my trip out to San Francisco, my father's health failed dramatically, and on December 9, 1981, he left us.

He was my mentor, my true and steadfast supporter, and with his voice ever in my ear, I had to carry on.

❋

By 1982 I was serving as a director of the American Bankers Association. The fact that I was the first *Nebraskan* to serve as a director seemed to make my appointment newsworthy:

> In national banking circles, Alice Dittman of Lincoln is regarded as a candid, articulate, spokeswoman. Some consider her one of the most astute women bankers in America. The past two years she has been a director of the American Bankers Association, the first Nebraskan to ever serve on that board. In Lincoln, Mrs. Dittman, president of Cornhusker Bank, seems to prefer a low profile. She takes quiet pride in having been the first female bank president in Lincoln.
>
> - THE LINCOLN JOURNAL-STAR

I quite enjoyed the new challenges presented by sitting on the national board. As to "first Nebraskan" and "first woman", I found them equally satisfying.

Things were going well at the bank, and I was always pleased when area newspapers took note of it.

> Although her banking career spans more than three decades, Mrs. Dittman continues to work hard to maintain her bank's growth record; since she became president, its assets have shown an average annual growth rate of 15 percent. Cornhusker Bank had assets of almost $24 million on December 31, 1982. This suburban bank has been in its new building at 11th and Cornhusker Hwy since September 1979. She takes pride in being an involved citizen.
>
> - THE LINCOLN JOURNAL-STAR

Newspapers took note of some of our innovations at the bank and cautiously referred to them upon occasion. We blazed a new trail for customer convenience by adding automatic teller machines (ATMs) at some of our locations in 1981. We took a bit of ribbing for adding that bit of technology for dispensing cash unattended. Banks in general are impatient to see an immediate response to their innovations, and when a month after installing the machines ours had made a grand total of seventeen transactions, it seemed to many that automatic tellers were a great big flop.

I was president of the Nebraska Electronic Transfer System at the time, an organization formed to support the launch of the new technology. Some of our committee members were embarrassed. Others began to complain. The only thing I could do was counsel 'patience'. I told them it was a solid innovation, and that if we dropped ATMs now, we'd just have to scramble to add them back in a year down the road when our customers began to demand them.

And sure enough, once people discovered the convenience of getting cash at any time, day or night, even on the weekends, our drive-through ATMs were rarely empty.

In 1991 we introduced a telephone service we called "Ask the Kernel". It used an automated voice-response system that early on handled 400 calls a day.

In 1994 we started doing check imaging—**the first Nebraska bank to do so**. Suddenly we were able to process an **average of 35,000 items per day**. It was a marvelous leap in productivity.

I do remember many of the staff being incredulous at the very idea of check imaging. Since the beginning, we had mailed the actual canceled checks back to the customers each month. But now we sent photocopied pages, with multiple check images on 3-hole punched pages. No more boxes of loose checks, just a nice, tidy, 3-ring binder. It went over well.

Amid all these changes, we were among less than 3% of the banks our size in the country to begin offering personal banking by computer. In 1995, when only 35% of households had a personal computer, we began to offer banking information on the worldwide web.

The technology inroads we were making at Cornhusker Bank prompted one of my favorite articles, with a title that reveals all the skepticism with which many bankers greeted technology.

INTERNET, SCHMITTERNET!
(GO AHEAD, PROVE ME WRONG)

It was written by Paul Nadler and appeared in the June 25, 1996 issue of *American Banker Magazine*.

> Ask two community bankers what they think of the Internet and you're likely to get two quite different answers.
>
> Some think having a World Wide Web site is mandatory today for the community bank.
>
> Others say: "Why be among the first? Let others pay the price of experimenting. We'll jump on the bandwagon when it becomes profitable to do so."
>
> I tend to be on the nay-sayer side. I think that much of our technology is solutions looking for problems.
>
> And many bankers who have taken first steps on the Net agree with me. Their Web pages are just places to advertise their services and, at most, provide depositors with balance information and other data. Customers can't even pay bills through these sites, or move money from one account to another.
>
> But Nebraska banker Alice Dittman says Internet skeptics like me are shortsighted.
>
> Ms. Dittman, president and chief executive of Cornhusker Bank in Lincoln, heads the electronic delivery steering committee of the American Bankers Association's 110-member Community Bankers Council. She writes:
>
> "The Internet allows any institution to market its

services and gain exposure in our communities. A larger competitor's presence on the Internet should be no less a concern to our bank than if we found the bigger rival trolling for customers via ads in our local newspaper.

"Many community bankers have already developed Web sites on the Internet and consider it a wonderful move. True, community banks can't pour the kinds of dollars and resources into technology that large banks can. But there's no reason for community banks to wait indefinitely or consider themselves non-candidates for technology leadership.

"Because many people assume that smaller banks are sleepier and less sophisticated than their larger brethren when it comes to technology, community banks that choose to wait do so at their own risk. Internet users tend to be more educated and more affluent than typical consumers and are ripe for the picking by larger banks and nonbank competitors.

"A presence on the Internet reaches those consumers, as well as younger folks (who one day may become the customers of our dreams), and it also puts employees on notice that the bank expects to keep up with the times and the tastes of its changing markets.

"I'm convinced that community banks must keep an open mind about where technology will fit at their banks. In many cases, we can be more nimble in implementing new technologies, which is an advantage in today's world of warp-speed technological change."

Letters like this made me want to take a second look at how banks are using the Internet so their customers can do from home what formerly involved a visit to the bank. I will report on some of these developments next week in this space.

It was most often the big banks I felt we needed to keep pace with. I've always said I prefer to play tennis with someone who can beat me, and that carries over into my work. Matching oneself against another of equal or lesser skill does nothing to promote growth or improvement. So when I saw effective technology being put in place, it was important to me to do the same. Of course, it meant adapting a large-scale process to our smaller operation. But that was just a matter of logistics.

I've always been proud of our bank's
leadership in technology.

Throughout the 80's and 90's these kinds of innovations were typical of Cornhusker Bank's culture, and were largely responsible for the fact that five years after the *San Francisco Chronicle* first forecast the demise of our community bank, we were going stronger than ever.

ALICE M. DITTMAN MAKES IT BACK TO S.F. AGAIN
Donald K. White |Banquet Circuit column — San Francisco Chronicle
WEDNESDAY OCTOBER 2, 1986

Welcome back, Alice M. Dittman. She is the president of Cornhusker Bank in Lincoln, Neb., and is attending this week's convention of the American Bankers Association at Moscone Center.

Five years ago, when the bankers last convened here, I predicted that under deregulation, there would be little need in the future for the likes of a Cornhusker Bank.

I suggested that Dittman probably was attending her last bankers' convention.

What with 14,500 commercial banks in the U.S., the trend obviously was to bigger and bigger banks and the demise of small banks.

Dittman and her bank are alive and well.

"I just wanted you to know that our bank is hale and hearty," she told me. "I am proud of the growth record of the Cornhusker [Bank]. Over the past 11 years we have averaged 15 percent a year compounded annually...It does give me the feeling that there is a 'niche' for a small commercial bank in the grand scheme of things."

The records show that the Cornhusker Bank has avoided the pitfalls of many another small bank in the mid-Plains that bet it all on agriculture.

The $40 million-in-assets bank has only 6 percent of its loan portfolio in agricultural loans, a solid 12 percent in commercial real estate loans.

Dittman assures me that she has every intention of coming to the next ABA convention in San Francisco. That one's scheduled for 1991. ¤

Naturally, I made certain when yet another five years passed and American Bankers were again gathering in San Francisco, I made my presence known to Mr. White.

CORNHUSKER BANK: RIDICULE IS NOT IN ORDER
Donald K. White | What's Up — San Francisco Chronicle
OCTOBER 6, 1991

Alice M. Dittman is back in town. Who, you may ask, is Alice M. Dittman?

How soon you forget. I wrote about Dittman 10 years ago this month. I wrote about her five years ago, too.

In 1981 I suggested rather strongly that the curtain was coming down on Dittman's act as well as on the roles of several thousand other bank presidents like her. She is the president and chief executive officer of Cornhusker Bank of Lincoln, Neb.

Ten years ago, there were 14,500 commercial banks in the U.S., which, I said then, "is about 14,000 more than a sophisticated economy needs. Is there really a need for Cornhusker Bank in the grand scheme of things?"

Shows how much I know.

Dittman's bank not only survived, it thrived, unlike many other small, medium and big banks that bellied-up in the last 10 years, were taken over by regulators or were merged.

Five years ago, when Dittman was in San Francisco for the annual convention of the American Bankers Association, she called me to report that "Cornhusker Bank is hale and hearty."

Now, with the ABA convention in town again this week, I feel obligated to do an update on Cornhusker Bank, an institution that I once claimed was unnecessary.

"We had $40 million in assets five years ago," Dittman said when I phoned her last week before she packed up her bags for the trip to the City. "We now have $82 million."

That impressive growth has not been at the expense of quality of loans, a trap that too many overly ambitious bankers have fallen into.

"A lot of big banks are losing money," Dittman said. "Our return on average assets has been more than 1 percent, at least in the last 20 years, and our loan losses average a quarter of 1 percent, which is a traditional norm for us. This year promises to be our best year ever."

Cornhusker Bank didn't achieve its robust balance sheet by going into a defensive crouch, loading up with government bonds and cutting back on lending, a strategy being used by many bankers who have been burned by the commercial real estate loans fiasco in many parts of the country, including California.

Nebraska's strong economy—it has one of the lowest unemployment rates in the nation—has encouraged Dittman to bring the bank's loan portfolio up to $46.7 million as of June 28 from $38.1 million a year earlier.

As chief executive officer of the bank, Dittman is in the catbird seat when it comes to shareholder support. She and her family own control of the stock.

"Our dividends are minimal," she said,. "We prefer to plow the money back into capital, surplus and undivided profits."

Her reference to plowing is apt, since Dittman is a farmer when she's not running Cornhusker Bank from her office overlooking Cornhusker Highway in Lincoln.

Naturally, she grows corn on her 150 acre spread, as well as milo and alfalfa. This year has been a good one for her farm, too. Crops have been abundant, she said.

When not being a banker or farmer, Dittman sharpens her tennis game and travels.

A widow who turned 61 last week and has been running the bank for 15 years, she describes herself as being "in pretty good shape on the court and up to a strenuous hike across a mountain range in New Zealand," a trek she made last year.

But Dittman's principal interest, aside from her three grown children, is Cornhusker Bank and the future of small banks generally.

"There are still [in 1991] over 12,000 banks in the U.S., and I think this diversity of management styles and the broad ownership of bank stock give our country a strength that perhaps countries with a very limited number of banks might not have in times of adversity," she said. [Editor's note: As of September 8, 2021, there were 4,951 commercial banks in the U.S.]

Dittman isn't fazed by predictions that the advent of interstate banking will hasten a decline in the ranks of small banks.

"I've never been concerned about interstate banking," she said. "There will always be a niche for smaller banks willing to compete with the giants."

Dittman's career was pretty much influenced by her heritage. Her father was an Oklahoma banker who sent her to the University of Nebraska, where she earned a master's degree in finance before going on to Harvard for courses paralleling the MBA program "in the days before they let women into the business school."

While Dittman will attend most of the banker's convention sessions, she's not much into the wining and dining that goes along with such gatherings.

"Anything good playing in town?" she asked me. I told her "Cats" was at the Golden Gate.

"Oh, I've seen it twice," she said. "In London and New York."

The president of Cornhusker Bank, clearly, doesn't fit the image of cow-town banker. ¤

Cow-town banker? Farmer? I don't mind that. It sounds like the kind of banker who would feel right at home in a fringy jacket.

*I never pass up an opportunity to spend time
on the family farm north of Lincoln that my
son Doug now owns and operates.
Here, the bluestem prairie grass is taller than I am.
The serenity I experience on the farm is second to none.*

Strawberry Park Resort
in Pahang Darul Makmur Malaysia

Nine

As Mr. Wright noted in the last of his three *San Francisco Chronicle* articles, I am a seasoned traveler. I remember 1992 in particular when I managed to hit six continents. That was the same year I became certified in scuba diving.

I've ridden camels on the desert with my children and grandchildren, taken a dawn balloon flight over the Serengeti plains, walked ancient Mayan ruins, trekked the mountaintop trails of New Zealand, and kissed Ireland's historic Blarney Stone. I've stood transfixed at the foot of Egypt's remarkable pyramids and contemplated a sphinx or two.

That Blarney Stone memory makes me wince a bit in retrospect. Some of my grandchildren accompanied me on that particular trip to Ireland, and when we visited Blarney Castle outside Cork, I announced that we weren't leaving until everyone had kissed the stone.

Kissing what some call the Stone of Destiny isn't just a matter of walking up to it, bending over a bit, and planting a kiss. The stone is suspended in the battlements of the castle wall high above the ground. One is only allowed to kiss the revered stone by turning one's back to it, resting the hips on a rail, and bending backward over the open space to essentially reach upside down to kiss the stone.

Over the years they've made safety adjustments to the area, and put bars below the open space so that if you lose your balance, you can't possibly fall to the ground. Still, as you are poised in that odd position, you can see the ground far below, and it can feel quite perilous.

We had a lot of laughs and gasps as each of us managed the feat. Then it was the last nervous grandson's turn, and he balked. I knew it was entirely safe, and that he'd regret it if he was the only one who didn't kiss the stone and earn his portion of eloquence, as the legend goes.

I didn't stop egging him on until he finally set himself in the opening and lowered himself to buss the stone. As he clambered up, another of our party whispered to me, "Oh my, he's terribly afraid of heights, you know. They make him nauseous." I immediately felt both horrible and horribly proud.

Those busy decades when my children were in high school and college gave us a number of opportunities to see the world. Dawn, John, and Doug were great travel companions. And later, when my grandchildren were old enough, I took them along, too. My one caveat worked out well. If Ganya (that's what they call me) wasn't having fun, we'd not go again. Somehow they managed to keep the fun times rolling.

My children and I made one early trip that will always invoke an involuntary shudder whenever I think of it. For a number of years I had wanted to travel to Russia, so when things opened up enough over there, I made sure my young-adult children's passports were current and off we went.

Everything about the country was fascinating—sometimes in a

good way, sometimes not. It was winter, and Moscow in the snow has a storybook look all its own.

With Doug, Dawn, and John in Moscow

We visited businesses, homes, historic sites, everything we were allowed to see, conscious the entire time that we were being watched. But nothing was intrusive, until we got to the airport for our return flight.

As we waited in line, we heard bits and pieces of scuttlebutt from other passengers regarding a coat hanger which had gone missing from a local hotel closet. Evidently travelers were being interrogated informally regarding the whereabouts of the errant hanger.

It was a simple wooden clothes hanger. Not gold or platinum or encrusted with priceless jewels. Just a coat hanger. We tried not to laugh at the absurdity of it.

Then, with no warning, my son John was pulled from the group and taken into another room. I was told to go on to the boarding area with Dawn and Doug, and John would join us after they'd asked him a few questions. I was not to know what those questions were or why they were being asked. I was merely to leave my son in their hands. On Russian soil.

I think not. I planted my feet outside that door and did not budge until at last John emerged, unscathed. Needless to say, we were miles into the air before my heartbeat finally slowed.

I truly loved our adventures. Especially the ones with my grand-children. I'd hear them cry, "Ganya! Look at that castle!" or "Ganya! Watch out for that crocodile!" Whatever the excitement, it was sure to result in a story that would continue to be resurrected around the holiday dinner table over the coming years. I never had to carry through on my warning—the one threatening no more trips if Ganya wasn't having fun. Those children and grandchildren filled my memory bank so full of fun and folly that I've little room for any-thing else. I treasure those memories like none other.

We look as if we've ridden camels all our lives. I'm on the left, with Carson, his mom Dawn, and Doug's son Nelson touring Egypt's great pyramids.

My seven grandchildren, long before it occurred to me
they might be the very best travel companions I could wish for.
Their parents, John, Dawn, and Doug,
were very special travelers, too!

Exploring Machu Pichu

*I've enjoyed a number of trips with this great
Colorado traveler and friend, Mary Ann Davis.*

Marveling at glaciers

On safari, before witnessing an attack on a wildebeest.
Behind me, my son John, twins Grant and Gregory,
with Carson and my daughter Dawn.

CORNHUSKER
B A N K

Ten

Over the seven decades since my parents first moved the Davey bank to Lincoln and christened it Cornhusker Bank, we've seen steady, reliable growth. Our seven branch banks ringed the city, making banking at Cornhusker easily accessible from all corners of Lincoln. And then we planted a branch in Omaha. My father was a visionary, but I wonder if even he could have envisioned this kind of expansion.

It even seemed to surprise some writers for the *American Banker* magazine whose business it was to follow banking evolution. In issues as late as 1998 they were still warning of the demise of community banks. They said things like, "Will Cornhusker Bank be one of the banks left in 2008? In the current environment, no bank, widely or closely held, can say with certainty that it will exist as an independent entity beyond maybe a year's time."

In the 1990s, so many banks were consolidating, or merging with bigger banks, that many expected us to do that, as well. But as one article concluded, "small firms can coexist with large—especially if the small are nimble."

What a great word that is. Nimble. I believe that's exactly what we are at Cornhusker Bank. We're small enough to implement new ideas quickly, to change with the needs of the community we serve. So yes, we're nimble. It's allowed us to stay strong in Lincoln and even add a branch in Omaha, which we hope will be the first of several.

A few years ago I was interviewed by *Silicon Prairie News* and was asked what was my favorite thing that I had built. I answered, "when you start work in a bank that only has half a million dollars in total assets, and over the past 65 years see it grow to $580 million, and see the bank occupy a new 55,000 square foot headquarters in 2017, that has to be my favorite, because of the jobs we provide and the customers we have helped grow their assets."

I take pride in our growth, and I know that today's success that was built on the shoulders of my parents is now bolstered by the insights of its current president, Barry Lockard, and the senior leadership team. About four years ago Barry launched an *Emerging Leaders Program* in the bank, and as I see it, the program exemplifies the fact that we are *"committed to your success"*, the bank's motto. It's not just the clients' success, it's the employees' success, as well.

But on an even larger scale, it's the success of the community and the state to which we're committed. From *One Day Without Shoes*, to *Leaders Are Readers*, to *Ventures in Partnership*, and General Colin Powell's *America's Promise*, our bank has continued to urge both employees and clients to participate in projects that underpin the good-heartedness of both Lincolnites and Nebraskans.

For me, that good-heartedness began with my parents. I recently came across a newspaper interview where a client of my father's told a story about the "goat lady". It seems that Karl Witt, a retired director of Cornhusker Bank, was in the midst of building a housing development to improve north Lincoln when he ran into a roadblock. One lone holdout would only move if Witt's firm bought her property and paid the cost of moving her belongings—including her goats.

According to his own account of things, Witt went to my father and said, "Can the bank loan me the money for this?"

Well, my dad said, "Nope, that's not a bankable loan." Then my father proceeded to lend Witt the money out of his own pocket and didn't even require a signature.

Those are the stories that my executive team—Ken Ward and Jim Mastera—and I tried always to remember over the years. It was a mindset that ruled our dealings with both clients and employees.

We three made a great team, and those two fine fellows never failed to support me in what I liked to call *"Mrs. Dittman's Soon-To-Be Famous Management by Amazement"*. That's a long-winded title for the simple fact that I'm always amazed at what people can accomplish when you just give them the opportunity. It's probably why over the course of twenty-four years at the helm, I only lost two officers to other banks.

Oftentimes over the years, newspaper advertisements for the bank would conclude with our tagline which read:

> *Cornhusker Bank remains the oldest family owned bank, demonstrating stability, soundness, and investing in the future growth of the community, its valued customers and associates throughout its long history.*

Now, as seen on our website www.cornhuskerbank.com, we post a much shorter tagline: *Doing life together.*

The tagline sits alone, underscored by a line describing our simple core values:

> *Own it. Care deeply. Deliver the "Wow" experience.*
> *Build positive relationships.*

In a paragraph at the bottom of the same page, one phrase jumps out: *We want to see you grow and prosper.* Nothing could be more true, and nothing could make my parents more proud.

Eleven

I had never thought much about what it might feel like to reflect upon a life's work. Now that I have both feet firmly planted in my ninety-first year, I find reflection happens more often than one might think.

While memories of awards and accolades do bring a smile, I find it can be the small things that actually carry the glow of accomplishment for me. That's how it is with the informal loans I often made over the years.

Each time I moved to a new office and began to organize a new desk, I made sure that the first thing I did was stock the top drawer with envelopes. They weren't ordinary business envelopes, but were smaller, like the kind that would carry a greeting card.

And they were never empty.

Each envelope held a few bills—perhaps $100, perhaps more— taken from the "bank of Alice Dittman".

Every time I found an opportunity to draw one of those envelopes from the drawer, I gave a prayer of thanks that I'd stocked it well. It was never the bank's money, just some of my own I found I could spare. Then, when a customer sitting across the desk from me couldn't manage to hide the stress they were feeling, or expressed fear of some sort over a financial burden they carried, I had something I could offer. Something that might alleviate that stress even for a moment.

In some cases there wasn't a traditional loan the bank could make in that particular client's situation, or it may have been that the client would have to take some further steps before they could be approved. And that could take time.

A small loan from the "bank of Alice Dittman" was often all it took to soften the anxious looks on their faces. With the fear and stress somewhat lessened, many were able to see more clearly that a solution was possible, that their difficult situation didn't have to be permanent.

I have no idea how many desk drawer loans I made over the years, and it truly doesn't matter. What matters is that the people who received those envelopes saw them as a turning point, a catharsis—a stepping stone. At least that was my hope.

They were a stepping stone for me, as well, because they were the catalyst for a project I launched in my retirement. A project I called *Alice's Integrity Loans*.

It was important to me that the loans awarded through this project would be given not based on the client's ability to pay it back, but upon the client's character. The client's integrity. Hence the name.

Over a period of three years, I seeded the project with one million dollars of my personal funds. I'm thrifty by nature, and thanks to some investments I've made over the years, I was able to contribute what to me seemed a significant sum. I can't express what a joy it is to have done that, to have given back in that way.

The loans were to be small—up to $5,000—the kind of thing a woman could buy a sewing machine and fabric with, if setting up a small cottage business was her goal. Or a pushcart and serving pans for a woman bent on catering. It was a modest sum that could support a modest dream. Because dreams don't have to be grandiose. A modest dream that fills a need or supports a passion is just as valuable to that individual as a desire to build the world's largest airline fleet is to another.

It was important to me that inability to obtain other credit previously would not stand in the way of obtaining a microloan from the Integrity Fund. We lent to individuals who had been through bankruptcy or even an addiction, if they could explain why that was behind them. We viewed their application in terms of character, capacity, commitment, and capital. If they needed a small loan to help their business grow, we wanted to be there with that stepping stone.

A beauty shop owner who wanted to expand her operation by one station heard about the program and came to us. She would need a chair, a sink, and plumbing. She already had the counter space in place. Another shopowner just needed an infusion of cash to purchase inventory before Christmas. In both cases, the Integrity Fund met their needs, and brought them one step closer to fulfilling their dream.

I often wonder how many dreams I've heard over the years.

One fellow came into the bank a couple of decades ago and showed great enthusiasm for his plan to build a chain of coffee houses. I'm embarrassed to recall that, while I didn't outwardly scoff at his idea, I held serious doubts about its viability. How could he sustain a business whose one goal was to sell a beverage people could already get at any restaurant in town? And drive-thru coffee shops? Really?

Fortunately, I lobbed the idea to another bank officer who had greater foresight than I in evaluating the fellow's idea. Now every time I see one of his successful establishments, I think of that young entrepreneur and silently compliment him on his innovative genius.

Time and again I've discovered that accidental timing can be the gift that ignites a new endeavor. In earlier pages I introduced Karl Witt and his difficulties with the "goat lady" holding up his project. That time, my father collaborated with him to solve the problem. Years later it was my turn.

The whole thing came about because of a chance invitation I received to attend a Merrill Lynch private seminar in downtown Lincoln. In that evening meeting I was introduced to a new type of building venture that could reap tax credits for investors. It captured my interest. Afterwards I asked the presenter where this project would be located. "New Jersey," was her reply.

The woman's presentation for whom she was seeking investors had been most convincing. Compelling, even. But why, I thought, send our money out of state? Why not mount a similar building project right here in Lincoln that would accomplish even more: improvements to north Lincoln, low-income housing for the elderly, and tax credits for local investors?

All it took was a word to builder Karl Witt, a nudge toward investor Ross Hecht and nine others—and my willingness to attend that evening session after a long day at work. The result was Aspen Haus.

How fortunate we would be if we all had perfect foresight, if we all could see "three acts" down the road even though the overture has just begun. How different our choices might be.

But our thinking is often clouded by our experience, or lack thereof, to the extent that we can't comprehend a solution that's being spelled out for us. I remember a certain banker who was bemoaning the fact that he'd love to include a businesswoman or two on his board of directors, "but Alice, there just aren't any," he said. When I casually mentioned to him that probably fifty percent of his depositors were women, I saw no gleam of understanding in his eyes. He'd decided there couldn't possibly be any women qualified to sit on his board and he wasn't going to bother looking.

And isn't that just the way we humans react? We've already closed our minds to the possibility that something might work, so we don't recognize the most brilliant solution even when it's laid out before us.

There are so many ways a person can manufacture their own stumbling blocks. I remember my first day as a post-graduate student working in the Davey Bank. It was 1953, and I had just been formally introduced to the fellow I would be working alongside. Some of his duties would now be mine. I was surprised to see that for some reason he just couldn't handle the fact that a woman might be his professional equal. In my mind's eye I can still see him as he threw his keys on my desk and walked away. He never returned to the bank.

What if I had made that experience into a stumbling block? What if I thought he had a valid point—that a woman had no business doing what he considered a man's job? It's possible an experience like that could have made me feel less assertive in the future. That would have been a monumental impediment, and I thank my youthful enthusiasm for allowing me to remain open to the possibility that working side by side with a male counterpart can be a strong, productive, congenial collaboration.

As I think about possibility, I realize it's now my grandchildren I watch for signs that they remain open to possibility. Whether it's an opportunity to improve their way of life, elevate their status in the business community, or lift someone else out of despair, will they see it? Are their eyes open?

In our travels—I've taken each of my grandchildren abroad—I've tried to capitalize on opportunities to demonstrate how important it is to watch for moments when their presence can make a difference in another's life.

I remember standing on a hillside in Ecuador, amid the shabby hovels of some of the poorest people I've ever seen. We were in the middle of the *favelas* in Rio. Among a group of children dressed in the mismatched tatters of street urchins was a little boy in the blazer and tie of a local school. His uniform was mended and patched, but clean, and I could hear his mother warning him not to do further damage to it.

Our guide questioned the mother and told us she was very proud that her son attended an academy that only took students who could excel in the schoolwork. Clearly, the boy's mother had sacrificed for him. Here she was, living in primitive conditions in a cardboard hut, but seeing to it that her son stayed in school, properly—albeit shabbily—dressed.

When we visited that boy's school, arranging for him to receive a new uniform was the very least we could do to support that young mother. We were given an opportunity to make a difference. How sad to think if we'd turned and fixed our gaze on the beautiful ocean view beyond instead of watching the children play, we might have missed the opportunity that was right beside us.

And what if we'd just waited too long? What if we thought about purchasing a uniform for the boy, but we stood there weighing the pros and cons just long enough for the mother and son to disappear down the alley before we found out the name of his school? What if we hadn't adjusted our itinerary to allow time for visiting the school?

That's the nature of opportunity. It's fleeting. Wait too long or hesitate just a bit and the moment to act is gone.

The same goes for opportunities to spend time with my

grandchildren. I was always aware that the window is brief, that they would get to the age where their careers and families overtook their lives and a trip abroad with their Ganya was no longer a possibility. So I seized the opportunity when the moments presented themselves, and made a lifetime of memories.

By the time grandchildren come along, you can even be a bit of a bad influence on them and get away with it. The youngest, Dawn and Jim's son Carson, tells his mother I am half kid and half grownup. That's a real compliment coming from a grandson.

Of my seven grandchildren, there is only one girl. John and Susan's daughter Allison was quite into tennis at one point, and I recall a special moment when we were talking about our passion for the sport. I had watched her play, and of course her parents attended many of her matches. Parents are so much more involved in their children's extracurricular activities these days, which seems to me to be a good thing.

I played tennis in high school for two years in Des Moines and through my senior year at Lincoln High. By 11th grade I was number one on the tennis team. I told Allison that I don't think my parents ever saw me play. She was horrified. But things just weren't so child-centric in those years.

I learned to play at the public courts, and the older kids would let me play with them if I helped roll the courts when we were done. There was a huge water drum we had to roll over the entire clay court, and then stripe it with lime. It was worth it to me, because I learned so much about tennis from the college players.

At the time it didn't seem like such a bold thing to do, asking those older kids to let me play with them. But perhaps it was. For most of my life I've felt willing to speak up. A person must. You have to speak up or you might as well not be there.

Oftentimes that takes persistence, but I've always been long on that trait. Just ask my junior high friends who accepted my challenge to keep two kites aloft for a full day. I pestered—or should I say persisted—just long enough for several to agree.

We arranged shifts so that two of us would be tending the kites at all times while the others went in relays to have lunch. A forecast for windy weather provided the opportunity, and my friends and I forged the plan and bolstered it with our determination.

At the end of the day we'd made ourselves proud. Our persistence had paid off, and how proud I was of our accomplishment.

You never know what impact your presence might have on others. You won't even be aware they're watching, but they are. The things you do not only shape their opinion of you, they may shape that person's attitude toward his or her own future possibility.

There wasn't any job in the bank that my family wouldn't do, or didn't do. No matter how small.

The willingness to do menial tasks isn't lost on others, either. I remember watching John Guenzel when he was president of the First Nebraska Trust Company. When another officer was giving a report, John got up and refilled the water glasses around the table. He was the CEO. He could have asked someone else to do it. But he did it himself.

It's a small thing. But they add up to big things.

The things you do when nobody's watching form the very definition of integrity. You make a decision very early whether to live and work with integrity. Or not.

For me, integrity is the most important element in any venture. It pleases me when I see my grandchildren behave with integrity.

I'll wager each of them can recite bits and pieces of my well-worn poem. At least I hope they can.

Isn't it strange how princes and kings,
and clowns that caper in sawdust rings,
and common people, like you and me,
are builders for eternity?

What did we actually make of what we were given?
Did we pay attention to that list of rules?
Did we misplace our bag of tools?

I suppose there are times in our lives when we've done both. I know I have. But if we are conscious of our acts, aware of whether they might build a wall or open a door, we can look back on choices well made.

Each must fashion, ere life has flown,
a stumbling block or a stepping stone.

I see now that at every stage of my life those words have been there, always leading me back to the commitment I made years ago to live my life with integrity, so that I might be the one who laid that very important stepping stone. The one you might be looking for.

Love,

Alice

PHOTOS *and* ARTICLES

I DO THINK IT MIGHT BE A
SECRET OF SUCCESS IN
NOT TAKING YOURSELF
TOO SERIOUSLY. IT ALWAYS
FELT GOOD TO MAKE PEOPLE
LAUGH ABOUT SOMETHING.

THE EASIEST WAY TO GET
TO KNOW PEOPLE IS TO
TALK TO THEM. I'D WALK
INTO A ROOM FULL OF MEN
AND MAKE A CIRCLE
AROUND THE ROOM.
I'D SAY, "HI," AND PUT
MY HAND OUT. IN 1975,
PEOPLE DIDN'T KNOW
TO PUT THEIR HANDS OUT,
AND I'D LEAVE IT THERE
TO SHAKE. IT'S IMPORTANT
TO INCLUDE OTHERS.
NOD OR SMILE.
THOSE ARE EASY TO GIVE
AWAY AND IMPORTANT IN
COMFORT BUILDING.

–ALICE DITTMAN

UNIVERSITY OF NEBRASKA COLLEGE OF BUSINESS ADMINISTRATION ALUMNI MAGAZINE
FALL 2004

INTEGRITY | INSIGHT | INGENUITY

Alice Dittman
A Woman of Firsts

"IF YOU DON'T DREAM, YOU WILL NEVER ACHIEVE."

The first woman chair of the Lincoln Chamber of Commerce, the first woman chair of the Bryan Hospital Board of Directors, the first female chair of the State of Nebraska Chamber of Commerce, the first woman president of Nebraska Bankers Association, and the first woman chair of the Community Bankers Association (a division of the American Bankers Association). Alice Dittman has been a pioneer in business in Nebraska.

"I think the acceptance I had in the Lincoln market area had a lot to do with my history with the University of Nebraska. I hope that I am a credit for the education I received there," Dittman says.

Dittman had a postgraduate year at Radcliffe before women were admitted to the Harvard Graduate School of Business. The Radcliffe students, however, did have joint classes with Harvard students.

"I felt I had a better business background than the women I was competing against. That was a real growing experience for me." Dittman finished her masters at Nebraska.

Dittman met and married Mark Dittman following her return to Nebraska from Radcliffe, when they were both working at her father's bank, Farmer's State Bank. After opening a bank elsewhere in the state and two banks in Missouri, Mark was diagnosed with cancer and passed away in 1975. Alice Dittman returned to Lincoln with three children and was offered the position of president of the family bank.

... continues on the following page

The lifesized portrait on the opposite page appears on a wall in Howard L. Hawks Hall, which houses the College of Business at the University of Nebraska–Lincoln. It's labeled "Alice Dittman - Notable Alumna"

PHOTO TAKEN BY CRAIG CHANDLER, DIRECTOR OF PHOTOGRAPHY
OFFICE OF UNIVERSITY COMMUNICATIONS

When Dittman took over as president and CEO of Cornhusker Bank in 1975, the value of the bank was $8 million. [At the time of this article] it is closer to $236 million. [Note: Today, in 2021, the value has exceeded $850 million.] Although not an entrepreneur in the pure sense of the word, she took the reins of a small rural bank and made it into an innovative regional bank. She had a long-range goal for the bank and for her role in the institution. Under her leadership, the bank was the first in the region to institute 24-hour access to accounts via telephone. It was the first bank in Nebraska to have imaging of bank statements.

Most of Cornhusker's business banking is with small to mid-sized entities. Being a smaller bank allows for quick individualized decision making: "We can literally make a decision at 9:00 and implement it at 10:00. Our approach to loans is to figure out how we can make the loan, rather than determine if the loan request fits some criteria."

She is satisfied with the growth of the bank, which has averaged 10% over the years. She explains that banks can't be run for both growth and earnings, but that with steady growth, the earnings will take care of themselves.

Cornhusker Bank is also known for its commitment to the success of local small businesses as evidenced by the full range of small business services it offers: SBA loans, merchant credit card sales, and full-service business insurance. Cornhusker Bank also offers a small business accounts receivable service designed to free up cash flow for small businesses. The bank's investment center provides retirement plans for small business owners and their employees.

Currently [2004], John Dittman is president of the bank and Alice Dittman serves as chairman. Dittman explains her success. "I got over being nervous. One thing you have to learn if you are going to be successful in business is to leave your comfort zone. I did well in my field, did my homework and continued to improve. I always had a three-year plan for myself and a seven-year plan for the bank. Another advantage I had were my contacts in the state, particularly Duane Acklie (CEO of Crete Carrier Co.)."

In 1987, Dittman was asked to join an advisory group for the [UNL] Center for Small Business at the College of Business Administration. She found the principles of the Center compelling. The concept of putting educational training to a practical use would result in success for the student and the program. The Center has since evolved into the Nebraska Center for Entrepreneurship. She has backed her belief in the Center with a financial endowment for the program.

Naturally, she has a strong interest in the fortunes of women entrepreneurs. "Disproportionately large numbers of businesses are created by women, and such businesses are disproportionately small."

Dittman is concerned about women-owned businesses and wonders if women are unsure about their business skills. Successful business owners have a clear objective in mind and the management tools to enforce appropriate gross margins on sales.

"Keep it simple. I always have a goal in mind and then try to anticipate the obstacles I will have to go around to get there. Determine the type of vehicle you need to achieve the goal. You don't need a tank to drive up the steps of the State Capitol building. Ask yourself, what is the right vehicle?"

Dittman is a believer in sports and athletics for women. "It is a great confidence builder for young women." She is an avid tennis player and golfer, still competing in both sports. She sees a dramatic increase in the confidence level of women, saying, "Women businesses are becoming increasingly professional, increasingly competent in their own abilities, increasingly goal oriented. But women must make some compromises in their professional life to fulfill the desire to do a truly excellent job in raising children, if they choose to have them."

Above all else, Dittman is a believer in people believing in themselves: "Nothing really happens unless you earn it. Enthusiasm," she says, "is essential to success. Nothing great is ever achieved without enthusiasm. If you or the people you work with don't have enthusiasm, the odds of success are greatly diminished." ¤

"Disproportionately large numbers of businesses
are created by women, and such businesses
are disproportionately small."
–ALICE DITTMAN

Alice M. Dittman Is Named President Of Cornhusker Bank

On Aug. 1, Alice M. Dittman will succeed her father, G.A. Frampton, as president of Cornhusker Bank, 2834 No. 14th St.

Alice M. Dittman

Frampton will remain as board chairman.

Mrs. Dittman will move to Lincoln from Kansas City, Mo., with her three children, Dawn, 15; John, 13, and Doug, 11.

Her husband, Marcus W. Ditt-man, died April 24, 1975. He was well-known in banking circles, and had most recently served as president and chief executive officer of North Hills Bank in Kansas City, Mo.

Mrs. Dittman received her Bachelor of Science degree at the University of Nebraska in 1952. A Harvard-Radcliffe Program and Administration graduate in 1953, she received her M.A. in Finance from the University of Nebraska in 1955.

She has been active in banking for 20 years, having been organizing officer of Central Bank, Central City, Neb. She participated in the organization of First National Bank of Richmond, Mo.

She has been continuously active as an officer and director of the Cornhusker Bank since its move to Lincoln in 1960, having served as vice president and board secretary.

Cornhusker Bank is the former Farmers State Bank of Davey, in operation there continuously from 1903 until its move to Lincoln.

Mrs. Dittman has served in various organizations in the Kansas City area, and most recently has served as president of Winding River Girl Scout Council, and as a member of the Speakers Division for United Way.

She is a member of PEO, AAUW, Beta Gamma Sigma and Alpha Xi Delta.

George Frampton's Favorite Quotes

Whenever I hear one of these familiar quotes, I hear them in my father's voice, as they were often spoken by him.

A penny saved is a penny earned.

Waste not, want not.

Make the rate fit the risk.

Use it up, wear it out, make it do or do without.

No one can borrow unless someone first saves.

You can't make a silk purse out of a sow's ear.

Don't worry about being able to pay the interest;
it's repaying the principal that is the problem.

Loans are made in good times and paid in bad times.

Shirtsleeves to shirtsleeves in three generations.

Borrow from Peter to pay Paul.

What you don't have in your head, you have to have in your heels.

Oh, what tangled webs we weave when first we practice to deceive.

Neither a borrower nor a lender be,
for a loan oft loses both itself and friend.

Two roads diverged within a wood, and I took the one
less traveled by, and that has made all the difference.

A rising tide lifts all boats.

Unto thine own self be true,
and thou canst not then be false to any man.

Trade two $50 cats for a $100 dog.

Watch your pennies and the dollars will take care of themselves.

It's hard to teach an old dog new tricks.

Business based on friendship is *not* good.
Friendship based on business *is* good.

Fish or cut bait.
(Make a decision and get going.)

Everybody's property is nobody's property.

Don't worry about the return *on* your principal,
worry about the return *of* your principal.

I just happened to be working at the bank in my University of Nebraska
College of Business Administration shirt when this
informal photo was snapped.

Executive of Distinction? Bank on it

FIRST FEMALE PRESIDENT OF NEBRASKA BANKERS ASSOCIATION
PAVED WAY, AND SPOKE OUT, FOR WOMEN WHO WOULD FOLLOW

It was the late 1970s and automated teller machines had been installed at a few Nebraska banks. Confused customers shied away from them. A month after their appearance, the ATMs had chalked up just 17 transactions, prompting one banker to wonder if the cash machines weren't just an expensive flop.

Alice Dittman, president of Lincoln's Cornhusker Bank, urged patience. She also was president of the Nebraska Electronic Transfer System, which had been formed to help with the push for electronic banking. Some of its members were complaining.

"If we drop them, we'll just have to start over again in a year—customers will demand them," Dittman told the group.

Her banking career began in 1948 with a summer job filing checks for First National Bank in Lincoln.

In 1952 she graduated from the University of Nebraska-Lincoln with a degree in business education. More degrees followed, including a master's degree in finance and management from UNL in 1955.

Dittman was the first female bank president in Lincoln. In 1975 she was named president and chief executive of Cornhusker Bank, a position she held through 1996.

In 1992 she became the first female president of the [Nebraska] Chamber of Commerce and Industry. A year later she was the first female president of the Nebraska Bankers Association, an industry group she'd belonged to since 1985.

"You have to earn it," Dittman said of her accomplishments. "You don't get to be president of the Nebraska Bankers Association unless you run a good bank."

Dittman also credits those who sometimes prodded her to step outside her "comfort zone," whether that involved speaking in front of people or taking up golf. Those steps were key to her advancement, she said.

It's advice she continues to offer men as well as women. And Dittman was outspoken in her march up the corporate ladder. In the pages of The World-Herald in 1991, she condemned sexual harassment— "a very common experience, particularly for young women entering the world of work"—and its damaging effect on business. Being the first woman, at times, was challenging.¤

–JANICE PODSADA

121

A Basketful of Firsts for Alice M. Frampton Dittman

1ST WOMAN PRESIDENT OF A COMMERCIAL BANK
IN LINCOLN OR OMAHA - 1975
CORNHUSKER BANK PRESIDENT
AND CHAIR OF ITS BOARD OF DIRECTORS

1ST WOMAN CHAIR
BRYAN HOSPITAL BOARD OF DIRECTORS - 1980

1ST WOMAN PRESIDENT
LINCOLN CHAMBER OF COMMERCE - 1988

1ST WOMAN CHAIR
NEBRASKA STATE CHAMBER
OF COMMERCE AND INDUSTRY - 1992

1ST WOMAN PRESIDENT
NEBRASKA BANKERS ASSOCIATION - 1993

FIRST WOMAN TO SIT ON THE
COUNTRY CLUB OF LINCOLN BOARD OF DIRECTORS - 1993

1ST WOMAN ROTARY NEBRASKAN OF THE YEAR - 1994

1ST WOMAN CHAIR
COMMUNITY BANKERS COUNCIL - 1997
(DIVISION OF THE AMERICAN BANKERS ASSOCIATION)

A favorite lunch spot of mine — The Hub Café.

"Keep it simple. I always have a goal in mind and then try to
anticipate the obstacles I will have to go around to get there.
Determine the type of vehicle you need to achieve the goal.
You don't need a tank to drive up the steps of the State Capitol
building. Ask yourself, what is the right vehicle?"

★

"The opportunity to head up a small bank that is 118 years old now
and has never been closed is a responsibility I take seriously."

★

"I always had a 3-year plan for myself,
and a 7-year plan for the bank."

★

"If you don't have a sleepless night or two over
some kind of worry, it's not normal."

★

"I always take the stairs," she says, and confides:
"When nobody's looking, I take them two at a time."

LINCOLN JOURNAL-STAR SEPTEMBER 19, 2019

2019 INSPIRE Woman of the Year
Honored by the Lincoln Journal-Star

Alice Dittman Inspires

**Former Cornhusker Bank CEO
named Woman of the Year
Lincoln Journal-Star**

Alice Dittman, former president and CEO of Cornhusker Bank, is this year's Woman of the Year.

Dittman received her honor Wednesday during the fifth annual *Inspire—Celebrating Women's Leadership Awards* at Pinnacle Bank Arena.

Dittman worked at the bank her family owned for nearly 40 years, serving as president from 1975-92 and then serving another 21 years on its board of directors. In 2011, she started a $1 million micro-lending program for entrepreneurs that's administered through the Lincoln Community Foundation. ...The event is hosted by the Journal Star and award winners are selected by the Inspire advisory board. ¤

2019
Journal-Star
INSPIRE
Woman of the Year

SALUTE TO LABOR

The faces of progress

| THE POLICE OFFICER | THE BANK PRESIDENT | THE AUTO APPRAISER | THE ELECTRICIAN | THE GOVERNOR |
| SUE CLARK, 52 | ALICE DITTMAN, 84 | DONNA KNICKERBOCKER, 50 | SHELLY DUBBS, 43 | KAY ORR, 76 |

Meet five women who wouldn't take a back seat to men

STORY BY JANICE POSADA | PHOTOS BY REBECCA S. GRATZ, KENT SIEVERS AND RYAN SODERLIN
SEPTEMBER 7, 2015 OMAHA WORLD HERALD

"You have to earn it."

That's true for workers of all stripes, but it's perhaps especially true for a group of Nebraska women who were among the trailblazers in jobs traditionally held by men.

It's how Alice Dittman, who uttered that maxim, became the first female president of any bank in Lincoln. She would have liked to have attended Harvard Business School in 1952, but couldn't because the graduate program didn't admit women.

It's how Sue Clark proved herself to male police officers who thought a woman couldn't do a man's job. In 1984, Clark joined the Omaha Police Department. She was one of a small number of female officers in the 600-person department.

It's how Kay Orr made history. She was elected governor of Nebraska in 1986, the state's first female governor and the first republican female governor of any state.

It's how Donna Knickerbocker won over customers skeptical that a woman could know anything about cars. She became an auto appraiser at Travelers Insurance in 2000.

It's how Shelly Dubbs eight years ago became the only woman in a class of 50 would-be electricians.

In 1948, when Dittman got her first banking job, as a summer worker, about 32 percent of women 16 or older were in the labor force, compared with 87 percent of men. Today, 56 percent of women older than 16 work, compared with 69 percent of men, according to the U.S. Labor Department's Bureau of Labor Statistics.

These five are barrier-breaking women.

END OF ARTICLE EXCERPT

Mortgage lending: Size doesn't equal profits

ABA

Banking Journal

FEBRUARY 1998

Try Keeping Up With Alice

Alice Dittman, chairman
of Cornhusker Bank
and the ABA Community Bankers
Council, makes things happen

Exclusive Results:
Community Bank
Competitiveness Survey

Cut your cash reserves

Try Keeping Up with Alice

STEVE COCHEO, AMERICAN BANKERS ASSOCIATION BANKING JOURNAL
VOLUME: 90. ISSUE: 2 PUBLICATION DATE: FEBRUARY 1998

In Alice Dittman community bankers have a goal-oriented achiever at the helm who just itches to improve things on all fronts

It was 1981 and the American Bankers Association Annual Convention had descended upon San Francisco. One of the local newspaper columnists, Don White, greeted the bankers by writing this skeptical observation:

"There are 14,500 commercial banks in the country, which is about 14,000 more than a sophisticated economy needs." White believed that the 1981 convention would be the "last hurrah" for many community bankers—and he singled out a few banks to bid them good-bye.

"Is there really a need for the Cornhusker Bank of Lincoln, Neb., in the grand scheme of things? Alice M. Dittman, the bank's president, will claim there is."

Dittman, now [1998] chairman of the bank, was not amused at the writer's predictions.

When the convention returned to San Francisco in 1986, White had to eat his words in print. "Welcome back, Alice M. Dittman.... Dittman and her bank are alive and well."

Some folks might have had White's column bronzed and hung on the wall like trophies. Not Alice Dittman. She's been too busy helping her $157 million-asset bank thrive—nor is it her style to gloat. Dittman is a doer—and the latest thing the 67-year-old has done is add still another item to a long list of "firsts" in her career—becoming the first woman to head the ABA's Community Bankers Council since its formation in late 1981.

That she is a woman is beside the point, really. Some folks—and some bankers—of both genders go through their lives and careers just kind of lumping along. That is not what Alice Dittman is about. Dittman is a born improver, one of those people who pick up an object and ask how it could look better, run better, be better.

She keeps this tendency in check through focus. Her long banking career has been ruled by a personal maxim: "One major thing and two minor things." That is, she believes in focusing on three goals a year that she will see accomplished if she has anything—and she will—to do with it.

"Alice is one of those personalities who sees the solution and doesn't see the problem," says George Beattie, executive vice-president of the Nebraska Bankers Association.

In spite of this focus, her radar is always on, alert to things that can be bettered, big and small.

The small things often come up on an impromptu basis. Case in point: A recent visitor announces that during his trip to Lincoln he wants to dash over the Kansas border. He has the goal of visiting every state before he dies.

Dittman considers this. As a goal-setter herself, she likes the idea of the lifetime goal, but just heading a car south to go over a border doesn't seem like half enough to her. Before the conversation is done, she has picked a goal for the traveler—Marysville, Kan., a site rich in the history of the old Pony Express—suggested the route and noted the likely travel time.

Bigger improvements that Dittman has put her hand to are so numerous that they defy summarization. But take technology as a facet that can be explored.

Anyone who thinks community banks can't ride the technology wave will have to think again after considering what Cornhusker Bank has done.

The bank was the first in Nebraska—indeed, one of the first community banks anywhere—to offer statement imaging for checking customers. Also, Cornhusker has its own network of more than two dozen automated teller machines—including one in a hotel—and offers 24-hour account information through its Kernel telephone service. The bank also provides access to banking information on its World Wide Web site (www.cornhuskerbank.com). It recently launched the Cornhusker OnLine Banking service, a PC-based service (operating via private line, not the Internet) that brings 24-hour banking service to customers, including bill paying, and permits use of popular money management programs.

Dittman has long been interested in the potential of technology to improve banking service. Between 1977-1986, she served on the board of the Nebraska Electronic Transfer System, which she chaired from 1983-1986.

"THE MUSCLE PART OF TOWN"

Lincoln is a city of contrasts. In places, especially around its towering limestone state capitol, it can be quite cosmopolitan—with trendy brewpubs and high-class eateries rivaling the fare of bigger cities, and with museums featuring such notables as Nebraska's "elephant"—the remains of a fossilized mastodon found in the area.

Yet Lincoln also has its more muscular side—the areas crisscrossed by Burlington Northern tracks that serve the city's heavy industrial and agricultural base

Cornhusker Bank's headquarters has been in what Dittman calls "the muscle part of town"—north Lincoln—since 1979. It's an appropriate location, because despite its agricultural-sounding name, the bank hasn't been in the ag lending business to a significant degree for years. North Lincoln was once considered the poor second cousin to the rest of the city, and in some ways, it was. Part of the problem was simply physical, the area being separated from much of the rest of the city by two streams, which were prone to flooding.

Several factors led to the district's revival. One was the creation of a dam that solved the flooding problem. Another was Cornhusker Bank's decision to begin branching in the area. The bank also made some no-interest loans to get things moving. Cornhusker Bank was seen as an institution that took an interest in north Lincoln. "People remember that kind of thing," says Dittman.

Most of Cornhusker's business is with middle-income people and with small to mid-sized businesses that value a community bank connection. The bank continues to add new services—it offers investment brokerage, financial planning, and a full line of insurance products, the latter through a bank-owned agency. It also makes use of secondary market loan programs—but its roots very much remain in local lending.

OUT OF HIS OWN POCKET

Alice Dittman's father, George Frampton, was a veteran banker who is remembered for his conservatism and integrity. Karl Witt, a retired director of Cornhusker Bank, recalls how his company, in the midst of building a housing development to improve north Lincoln, needed to strike a special deal with one holdout known as "the goat lady." She would only move out if Witt's firm bought out her property and paid the cost of moving her belongings—including her goats.

"I went to Frampton and said, 'Can the bank loan me the money for this?'" says Witt. "He said, 'Nope, that's not a bankable loan.' But he lent me the money out of his own pocket. And I didn't even have to sign anything for it."

Alice Dittman had a business-oriented education, first with a BS at the University of Nebraska right

in Lincoln and subsequently with an M.A. in finance and management from the same school. In between, she attended a graduate business program at Radcliffe, in the days before women were admitted to Harvard University.

She returned to the Lincoln area in 1953 to work in her father's bank—then situated in Davey, Neb., and known as the Farmer's State Bank—taking the post of cashier. During this time she married Mark Dittman, who joined the bank as well. With a very small staff, everyone did a bit of everything and that helped teach the couple the business.

CHILDREN, DE NOVOS, HARD WORK

They learned enough to start their own bank elsewhere in the state, Mark Dittman as president and Alice Dittman as cashier. The bank did well, but when George Frampton moved his Davey bank to Lincoln to capitalize on more growth opportunities, the couple sold their interests and returned to work at the newly named Cornhusker Bank. Alice Dittman began working part-time, as she had two small children to raise.

A year later, the family moved—now with three children—to Richmond, Mo., to start another bank on behalf of an investor group that came courting. Besides taking care of the family and helping out in the community, Alice Dittman spent a few days each month back in Lincoln, helping her aging father run Cornhusker.

In 1971, an offer to start another Missouri bank came. Then, shortly after making the move to this third de novo, Mark Dittman was diagnosed with cancer. He died in 1975, after a three-year illness. Alice Dittman accepted her father's offer to come back to the family bank as president and CEO.

Making it all work—family, business, community commitments—was a struggle demanding long hours, skipped vacations, and more. Her children, then 11, 13, and 15, took on increased responsibilities to help make the arrangement work.

Dittman was helped by many people in the bank as well. Notable among them are her two longtime lieutenants, K.R. (Ken) Ward and James A. Mastera, both executive vice-presidents responsible for operations and lending, respectively. Through much of Dittman's history with the bank, the three acted as an executive team.

Both Mastera and Ward attribute a big part of Dittman's success as a manager to what she herself calls, "Mrs. Dittman's Soon-To-Be Famous Management By Amazement." As she describes it, "I'm always amazed at what people can accomplish when you just give them the opportunity." Many speak of her willingness to give employees responsibility and the way that it frequently pays off for the bank.

STEADY GROWTH, WITH ATTITUDE

Inside what once was the parachute loft of a defunct air base that is now an industrial park in Lincoln is one of the loan customers that Dittman shows off with pride.

This is the Gene R. Bedient Co., makers of "tracker" organs. These are the massive organs one sees in large churches. The "tracker" is the mechanism that, manipulated by the keyboard, controls the flow of air through the huge metal and wooden pipes.

The occasion of Dittman's latest visit is the open house that owner Gene Bedient has called to unveil the company's latest creation—a tracker organ for Ohio University's chapel. The company has been in business for 30 years and yet this organ is only the 56th that it has produced. You don't produce tracker organs en masse.

In many ways, community banking, as Dittman practices it, parallels Bedient's organ business. "Community banks give high service to those that need it," says Dittman.

Likewise, Dittman sees banking as a deliberative affair.

"It's not a complicated business," she says, "and it shouldn't be. I have a balance sheet and a profit-and-loss statement every day. Together, that's a steering tool that makes banking an easy ship to steer. But it turns like a tanker, not like a speedboat."

"You've got to be clear in your mind that we, as bankers, must be good stewards of other people's money, first and foremost," she continues. Building an institution like Cornhusker Bank "has been a lifetime of effort" that comes along slowly but surely, like one of Bedient's organs.

The bank's growth has been slow and steady, Dittman says. It has averaged 10% asset growth for 22 years. Dittman believes this is best for the bank and its customers. Steadiness, for the customer, means the ongoing opportunity to maintain contact with management. "Sometimes an institution's memory bank gets lost in the transition between loan officers when a bank grows too fast," says Dittman. She points out that Cornhusker has lost only two officers to other banks in the 24 years she has been there.

It's a very personal philosophy of mine that I never try to manage our return; our goal has never been to maximize earnings," she explains. "We've done well, but it hasn't been the first priority."

She is satisfied if the bank is in the top quartile of community banks, because, she explains, you can't run a bank for long both for growth and earnings, and she has always been interested in seeing Cornhusker grow.

So it is not surprising that Dittman—and Cornhusker Bank— lend with a longer-term perspective than some.

"These are good times banking is going through right now," Dittman notes. "But they have not become a norm. My dad always said that 'Loans are made in good times and paid back in bad times.'"

Steadiness doesn't mean inflexible. Dittman has learned to adapt to changing times. For example, Lincoln has seen an influx of immigrants, particularly Asians, in recent years. That has required some adjustment in loan practices, she notes. Asian families often take on debt as a family—one home loan she recalls had six signers. But the bank helped get the family into their house.

Still, Dittman admits that sometimes being a conservative banker gets the better of her. One prospect came to her seeking a loan to start a chain of coffee centers around town. This was before such trendy shops were well known and Dittman simply couldn't see building a business around a single beverage that nearly any eatery in town served.

Fortunately for the bank, Dittman felt the prospect deserved a fair hearing, and so she referred him to another lender at the bank. Today the coffee house operator is one of the bank's customers.

THOUGHTS ON THE INDUSTRY

While she acknowledges that there have been divisions in the banking industry between large banks and small banks, Dittman thinks too much has been made of them.

"We are all community banks, regardless of size," she says. "You know, the CEOs at big banks get further away from their customers in their day-to-day responsibilities, but all bankers are in the same service business."

Dittman sees several priorities for community banks and hopes the ABA Community Bankers Council can play a role in addressing them.

One is bankruptcy. Dittman says she is concerned about possible efforts to reform bankruptcy laws.

What she calls the "permissive" issuance of credit cards also has her worried. As a small business specialist, she says, Cornhusker Bank has seen more and more aspects of small firms financed through plastic.

Another issue is the Financial Accounting Standards Board, setter of "generally accepted accounting principles," which banks have had trouble accepting of late. Dittman is very concerned about FASB's continued push for more and more uses of market-value accounting.

"FASB has a religious zeal that is, in some cases, nonproductive," says Dittman.

And then, there is financial modernization. Dittman is all for it. It's time to kill the thrift charter and merge the insurance funds, she says, and banks ought to have expanded flexibility. She's not just saying that for the sake of apple pie and motherhood, either. Dittman sees potential for community banks like Cornhusker in the limited blending of banking and commerce contained in pending House legislation.

MANAGEMENT IN TRANSITION

By now you should know that it's completely in character for Alice Dittman to go from floor to floor in her three-story headquarters by stairs, rather than wait for the elevator. "I always take the stairs," she says, and confides: "When nobody's looking, I take them two at a time."

Active as she remains with the bank and the Community Bankers Council, Dittman has half an eye

on retirement and management transition. She added the chairman title in 1993, upon the retirement of her nonbanker brother. In 1997, she turned over the presidency to her son John. (Her two other children, Doug and Dawn, do not work for the bank; she has five grandchildren.)

When she turns 70, she will retire, as the board's official retirement age is 70 and that has been observed by family and nonfamily members alike.

Art Knox, a director whose tenure goes back to the days of Dittman's father, has long admired Alice Dittman's leadership qualities, and expects the latest Dittman will continue the pattern. "John is a good leader himself," he says.

Following his mother doesn't faze John Dittman in the least. He's learned the business on the job. "I have plenty of time," he says. "I plan to spend a long period of time here, to make my own reputation. I have to earn that."

As for Alice Dittman, she has tried to make the transition as smooth— and plain—as possible. She "offices," as she puts it, in one of the bank's newer branches these days, so that John can occupy the president's office in the main bank. That way the transition is clear to customers.

True to her career form, Dittman intends to make a "success" of retirement. Given the remarkable experiences of her lifetime to date, who would expect any less? ¤

AK-SAR-BEN
COURT OF HONOR
2009

IT WAS A GREAT JOY TO SIT IN THE
COURT OF HONOR REPRESENTING
BUSINESS AND INDUSTRY
IN NEBRASKA

My children's grade school portraits

From left, my daughter Dawn, a former Director of Marketing for the Texas Parks and Wildlife Department, with her husband, Judge Jim Coronado, a past director of the State Bar of Texas; Krista with Doug at the top; John next to me with his wife Susan, an accomplished author of historical and inspirational fiction and nonfiction, with their twins Grant and Gregory; and in front of me, Mark and Allison. All four children belong to John and Susan. And yes, when all four were under the age of five and a half I babysat once—though I brought along a friend to help!

One year, after our bank's annual meeting, we
gathered my sports-minded grandchildren together
for this photo. They are such a wonderfully mixed bag
of smiles and smarts and savvy wit.

Family times never failed to bring smiles all around. My backyard was a favorite spot to capture my growing family.

Youngest grandchild Carson and only granddaughter Allison.

Above, surrounded by my barefoot bunch in Lincoln. Below, halfway around the world on safari with John and his twins, Grant and Gregory, and Dawn and her son Carson.

Above, my boys John and Doug.
Below, with my daughter Dawn and son John.

At left, traveling with Dawn at Strawberry Park Resort in Pahang Darul Makmur Malaysia.

Below, with Dawn's son Carson at his high school Baccalaureate.

Happy Grandparents Day!

Ganya, You're the best! Sending a Texas-size hug to you. Love, Carson

Above, at Strawberry Park in Malaysia.
Below, with my brother Bob Frampton at our
Florida tennis club in Punta Gorda.

My grandchildren proved to be great travel companions. As you can see, they made sure Ganya was having fun! Mark, my oldest grandchild, was the first to travel with me. Our visit to Ireland was a great success and he paved the way for the rest of my seven grandchildren to have their own trips with Ganya (me).

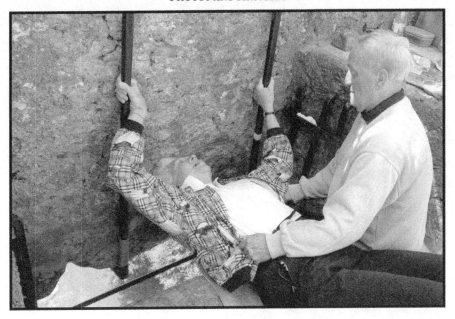

Yes, that's me kissing the Blarney Stone in Ireland.
Below, Grant and Gregory made our trip to Tanzania lively and memorable.

The best way to see the great pyramids of Egypt, I'm convinced, is on the back of a camel. Grandson Nelson may or may not agree.

Below, I have many great memories of this 1980s family trip to Cancun with my college-aged children.

Ecuador in 2007 with Allison, Dawn, and Carson,
was fascinating and fun.

Above, four of my grandchildren: Dittman cousins Allison, Andreas, Grant and Gregory. Below, Grant and Gregory are giving an illuminating FDIC presentation on cryptocurrency. Yes, they have educated their Ganya on the topic.

Above, with grandson
Andreas at the Standing Bear
sculpture dedication in 2017.

At the right, I was honored
to wear his letter jacket at
a family outing—if only
briefly.

My calendar always seems packed with business and social lunches.

happy 90th birthday

October 1, 2020

In spite of the Covid restrictions we had to observe, my children blessed me with a marvelous gathering of two hundred friends and family to celebrate my 90th birthday.

Each year I do a bit of cleanup for my mother's Meyer family gravesite at Wyuka Cemetery in Lincoln. My family interred there dates back to William Ferrell Hollingsworth, my great-grandfather. He and his wife, Emaline Hall Hollingsworth, were parents of my maternal grandmother Mary E. Meyer. She and her husband Nelson were my mother, Cecile Meyer Frampton's, parents.

William F. Hollingsworth was born in Vermillion County, Indiana, on January 20, 1837. He fought as a Union soldier with the Eleventh Indiana Volunteers, Company C, in the Civil War. His personal diary contains a stark account of the regiment's movements and in particular their participation in the Battle of Vicksburg.

152

Doug and Krista, Susan and John
with me at the Lincoln Community Foundation
Charity Award presentation.

I was thrilled and humbled to receive an Honorary Doctor of Laws from
Nebraska Wesleyan University in May of 2014.

NEBRASKA Fall 2004

Business

Alice Dittman
A Woman of Firsts

Chats with our Nebraska Electronic Transfer System (NETS) board and staff
were always educational and enlightening.

Above, I'm with Jim Abel and Lincoln mayor Mike Johanns
at one of our branch bank ribbon cuttings.
Below, a grand opening ribbon cutting for our Bethany branch.

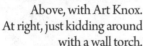

Above, with Art Knox.
At right, just kidding around
with a wall torch.

Each of these nineteen Cornhusker Bank officers had been with the bank an average of more than sixteen years when this photo was taken. Together, they represented more than four hundred twenty-five years of experience at Cornhusker Bank. It was gratifying to lead an organization that did so well at retaining its talent. Pictured with John and myself are Ken Ward and Jim Mastera. Behind us in no particular order are: Jeff Breunig, Mike Gardner, Kurt Grosshans, Laura Gyhra, Marilyn Horky, Sally Jacobs, Brian Johnson, Steve Lindgren, Mary Jo McClurg, Pauline Smith, Cheryl Socha, Tom Soukup, Dian Stoakes, Bob True, and Judy White.

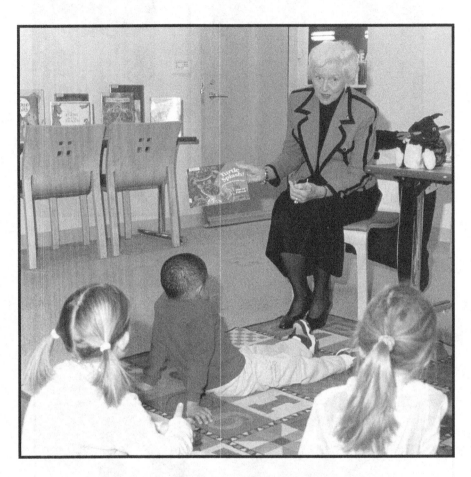

 Thank you for supporting
Leaders Are Readers
2003-2004

Alice Dittman
Cornhusker Bank
Leader Reader

Above, doing teller duty.

Below, having great fun riding around the park in Davey in a miniature Burlington Northern railroad car with my brother Bob. These train rides were a big hit during the bank's 100th anniversary celebration on August 24th of 2003.

I have always been grateful for
any opportunity to introduce
children to the concept of thrift.

Some of the Lincoln business executives who will be clowning around during the Star City Holiday Parade on Dec. 5: bottom row (left to right), **Jim Nissen, Bus Whitehead** and **Jerry Mapes;** second row, **Frank Hilsabeck, John Haessler,** and **Al Hamersky;** third row, **Duane Acklie, Alice Dittman, Burnham Yates** and **Chuck Heinke;** top row, **Dale Jensen, Lynn Wilson, Gates Minnick, Vern Roschewski** and **Rich Bailey.**

When they send in the clowns, look for 21 business executives

By David Swartzlander
Journal Writer

So you think your boss is a clown.

You might be right.

On Dec. 5, 21 executives of Lincoln firms will trade conservative three-piece suits for flamboyant, multicolored clown costumes, complete with pompons on pointy caps.

So much for power dressing.

They actually will go out in public wearing these custom-made costumes as they ride a San Francisco-type trolley in the Star City Holiday Parade.

Why will these business bigwigs paint their faces, don baggy pants and make fools of themselves on Dec. 5? That is what Dale Jensen's co-workers at Information Technology Inc. want to know.

"They ask me, 'Why do you want to do this on a Saturday when you do it every weekday?'" said the firm's executive vice president.

Rich Bailey, chief executive officer of Bailey, Lewis & Associates Inc., has his own theory.

"It gives everybody a chance to do something deemed totally unacceptable at any other time of year," he said. "We can look like fools and get away with it. And the ludicrous thing is that we pay $500 for this privilege."

Why?

"I go to bed every night wondering why I popped $500 to be a clown," said Jerry Mapes, chairman of Mapes Industries. "Since I'm sort of a clown anyway, I guess I decided to put it to good use."

There is a more serious, community-oriented reason for business leaders to clown around. They are parade benefac-

tors, for they each donate $500 to help pay for it. Their ranks include a financial consultant and executives from advertising, architecture, banks, a car dealer, an oil company, an insurance firm, a trucking firm, hospitals and various industries. The number of executive clowns increased by six this year.

"They have a riot," said Vickie Smith, chairman of the Executive Clown Corps committee. "They're really a neat bunch of people. They take time out and are real supportive."

Second year

This is the second year for the clown corps. Longtime funny faces will be identified by two large stars on their costumes, Smith said.

Most of those who were interviewed said they became clowns for fun and to promote a good cause, but some, such as Jensen, had ulterior motives.

"I'm a ham at heart," he said. "I always wanted to be, had a secret desire to be a clown."

Jensen's costume has some significance: It contains the royal blue and white corporate colors of Information Technology. Bailey told the costume maker just to put together something appropriate for him.

"Mine looks like all the other clowns got sick and threw up on it," he said. "It's a liver bio-green and chartreuse dotted with a few flecks of orange. I've never seen a necktie that bad."

Cassie Chandler, the official costume maker, had to use a full yard of fabric for Bus Whitehead's costume. When they send in the clowns, Whitehead, president of Whitehead Oil Co., will tower over all

at 6 feet, 9 inches.

All big

Whitehead's size led to a good-natured gripe by Mapes.

"They came and measured us and then made all the costumes the same," he said. "They were all made for Bus Whitehead."

Mapes seems to be the only one with the credentials to be a clown. He can juggle, you see, and he knows some magic.

"I can turn in to a tavern," he said. "That's my disappearing act."

Other executive clowns are Al Hamersky, architect with The Clark Enersen Partners; Vern Roschewski, president, First Federal Lincoln; Bill Smith, chairman, FirsTier Bank Lincoln; Gates Minnick, Lincoln City councilman and president of Du Teau Chevrolet; Paul McCue, general manager, Journal-Star Printing Co.; Frank Hilsabeck, vice president, Lincoln Telephone Co.; Jim Stuart, chairman and chief executive officer, National Bank of Commerce; John Haessler, president and chief executive officer, Woodmen Accident and Life Insurance Co.; Alice Dittman, president, Cornhusker Bank; Chuck Heinke, executive vice president, Havelock Bank; Jim Nissen, president, Vistar Bank; Jim Abel, president, NEBCO Inc.; Tom Smith, Smith Hayes Financial Services Corp.; R. Lynn Wilson, Bryan Memorial Hospital; Duane Acklie, president, Crete Carrier Corp.; Burnham Yates, retired head of First National Bank; and Bob Lanik, president, St. Elizabeth Community Health Center.

8A

JOURNAL STAR
Thursday, October 2, 2008

Comments? Questions? Call Richard Piersol, 473-7241
Page Design: Jamie Garbacz

MARKET WATCH

Dow Jones Industrials	-19.59	10,831.07
Standard & Poor's 500	-5.30	1,161.06
NASDAQ	-22.48	2,069.40
Russell 2000	-7.99	671.59

BUSINESS BRIEFS

Berkshire Hathaway to buy GE preferred

Warren Buffett's Berkshire Hathaway is buying $3 billion worth of General Electric preferred shares, as the diversified conglomerate is preparing to sell at least $12 billion worth of common stock to the public.

GE says Berkshire Hathaway Inc. will buy $3 billion of perpetual preferred stock in a private offering. Such stock carries a dividend of 10 percent and is callable, at a 10 percent premium, after three years. Berkshire also received warrants to buy $3 billion worth of common shares at $22.25 each over five years. GE says that the Berkshire funds will boost its cap-

BUSINESS

www.journalstar.com/news

Banker chides government

Lincoln business leaders gather to hear Fed economists.

BY RICHARD PIERSOL
Lincoln Journal Star

Between mildly optimistic presentations by Federal Reserve economists, who were in Lincoln on Wednesday on their annual tour of Tenth Fed District cities, the dean of Lincoln bankers, Alice Dittman, gave a quick summary of what she believes has put the U.S. economy at risk.

"Do you suppose there was a corruption of lending standards that was not only encouraged but promoted to boost the economy through new home production, which leads to new shopping centers and other ancillary businesses?" the chairwoman emeritus of Cornhusker Bank asked, not so rhetorically.

The implications of poor U.S.

financial management at many levels hung heavily in the air at The Cornhusker hotel, even as the Fed economists predicted less severe economic fallout in Nebraska than elsewhere.

That same evening, the U.S. Senate voted to rescue financial institutions from bad decisions and, presumably, the U.S. economy from the worst possible consequences.

Life is full of temptations, political, financial and otherwise, according to Dittman, who was among scores of local business leaders invited to the presentations.

"Remember 'a chicken in every pot?' she asked, recalling the campaign slogan of the luckless Herbert Hoover, not to mention his 'car in every garage.'

"A 'homeowner' in every house," she said, "without regard for the discipline it takes to buy a home and consistently make the payments."

Dittman was just warming up.

"The constriction of credit al-

Nebraska economy

Nebraska's leading economic indicator once again moved below growth neutral. The September Business Conditions index from a survey of supply managers dipped to 49.1 from August's tepid 51.2.

"Firms with ties to automobile production are experiencing downturns in economic activity. Nondurable manufacturing firms, especially food processors, continue to detail reduced economic activity," said Creighton University's Ernie Goss, who compiles the index.

legedly afflicting big financial institutions that are afraid to lend to each other — among the reasons given for the Senate's need to act — isn't a problem at Cornhusker Bank.

Its branches have signs that say, "Loans on Sale."

"It can't be more 'dear,'

'Credit is like fire: It can warm you or burn you. A lot of people got too close.'

— Alice Dittman, dean of Lincoln bankers

Dittman said.

The aforementioned mortgage-related credit ailments are infecting "the high fliers," she said.

Nebraska has had the good fortune to be insulated so far from the worst of the economic troubles brought down by others, according to Dittman and Omaha Fed Branch executive Jason Henderson, who described the state's economy as very resilient, slower than it was earlier this year but holding up much better than most of the rest of the nation.

That's thanks to the agricultural boom and, encouraged by the low value of the dollar, brisk exports.

And no thanks to the profligacy of the age, according to Dittman.

"Congress, in its wisdom, discontinued the deduction of interest payments on cars, so people finance cars through the equity on their homes, to extremes," she said. "Where does it end up? First mortgage, second mortgage, a charge card that ends up being a third mortgage. This has been going on for a long time.

"Credit is like fire: It can warm you or burn you. A lot of people got too close," she said.

Particularly angered by the collapse of Fannie Mae and Freddie Mac, the mortgage finance agencies created by Congress, Dittman says of them: "I don't understand who was watching or not watching."

"We've got to turn this around and teach thrift," she said, describing the joys of its practice.

"I feel very strongly (about it)," Dittman said.

Reach Richard Piersol at 473-7241 or dpiersol@journalstar.com.

Tell us about it

To give us business news tips, openings, closings or other suggestions, please write us at businessnews@journalstar.com.

"The Dean of Banking"
That title originated in a newspaper article and tickled me greatly.

THE LINCOLN STAR WEDNESDAY JULY 6, 1988

She's no ordinary banker
or chamber head

DON WALTON

The chairman of Lincoln's Chamber of Commerce lists tennis and banking among the hobbies on her resumé.

But don't be deceived. She's serious about both of them. She comes to play and plays to win, competing head-on with the men on the tennis court as well as in the bank boardrooms.

Alice Dittman is president and CEO of Cornhusker Bank.

This year she became the first woman to head Lincoln's Chamber, a predominantly male business organization comprised of almost 1,800 members.

One of her goals is to "make the chamber into a little more of an open and accessible personality."

"The chamber can be perceived as a stodgy organization of men in pinstripe suits. Obviously, I don't fit that image."

What image does Dittman fit?

Businesswoman, community activist, Lincoln and Nebraska booster.

"It's an exciting time to head the chamber," she says. "We're just coming off the strategic planning phase, the StarVenture year, and we're ready to fresh out the strategies.

"What we need are new and dynamic jobs for Lincoln. Not just blue or white or pink collar jobs, but new collar jobs. We need to be able to provide entry level opportunities that will keep young people here. We're losing them now."

And good jobs for people who are leaving the farm, too. And for those who already work here.

Lincoln's low unemployment figures are deceiving, Dittman says. "I think there's lots of underemployment."

Dittman is "very optimistic" about Nebraska's economic future.

"I do hope we give LB775 and LB270 time to work.

"Business wants a stable tax and work environment. It wants predictability. Employees want that, too. It means job security."

LB775 and LB270 are the legislative bills that contain Gov. Kay Orr's package of investment and employment growth tax incentives for business.

"I don't mean to be Pollyanna, but I really think we've got something going in Nebraska now—although I must admit I'm concerned every morning that I see clear skies.

"This drought can have a really negative impact. It will affect all segments of business in the state."

Dittman, who grew up in a banking family, has been president of Cornhusker Bank since 1975. She started as a cashier when it was the Farmers State Bank of Davey.

"You work very, very hard on a thin profit margin in banking. If a bank does well, it nets 1 percent on its assets. Forty percent of Nebraska banks in 1986 either broke even or lost money; the picture improved last year.

"But we have to be careful. You're loaning the depositors' money. You make every credit-worthy loan you can, but sometimes you do a person a favor by turning them down.

"You don't make a bad loan. But sometimes they turn bad for a variety of reasons—some of which are not the borrower's fault."

Once a week, when she can, Dittman takes to the tennis court to play the game she loves.

"I think I have more energy when I exercise," she says.

"I play with some of the fellows. They've made me a regular member of their group."

She finds enjoyment too in reading. And in 5:30 p.m. movies.

And sunsets.

"I'd match our Nebraska sunsets against anybody's mountains and lakes. They're spectacular. The Japanese business delegation that was here recently mentioned them."

NEBRASKA offers lifestyle advantages, too, she says.

"We get to look out at trees and grass, not just buildings.

"We have freedom and independence of space. I think that makes us easier to get along with and more willing to help each other."

Dittman, whose husband died in 1975, has three children, all in their 20s.

She lives "downtown" now, or at least close to it, high atop Sky Park Manor at 13th and J.

"It's fun. I have a great view of the Capitol. Did you know it was built to last 700 years? Just think of that. It's a real treasure. And I can watch the sunsets from up there."

Another real treasure in the eyes of Alice Dittman, too. ¤

Alice has thrived on the road less traveled

PHOTO COURTESY LINCOLN JOURNAL-STAR

Alice's
*Integrity*Loan Fund*

A woman of firsts
seeks to give others their start

STORY BY BAILEY LAUERMAN / PHOTOS BY JOHN KELLER
OCT 21, 2011 — L MAGAZINE

Alice Dittman is former president and CEO of Cornhusker Bank. Dittman continues to influence the community, in 2011 establishing the $1 million Alice's Integrity Loan Fund at the Lincoln Community Foundation to help budding entrepreneurs and small business owners. Dittman was the first woman to preside over the Lincoln and Nebraska Chambers of Commerce and the Nebraska Bankers Association as well as the Community Bankers Association. She was also the first woman to chair the Bryan Memorial Hospital board and to be elected to the Lincoln Country Club board.

John F. Keller

THOSE CLOSE TO ALICE DITTMAN know her as a pioneer - blazing trails others have not yet taken with class and grace. She takes time to listen and learn, all the while teaching others how to lead with integrity. And most recently, she took her life's work as a banker and translated it to an unprecedented program for Lincoln entrepreneurs - with an emphasis on women and minorities.

Former president and CEO of Cornhusker Bank, Alice, age 81, is well known for her many firsts. She was the first woman to preside over the Lincoln and Nebraska Chambers of Commerce and the Nebraska Bankers Association as well as the Community Bankers Association (a division of the American Bankers Association). She was also the first woman to chair the Bryan Memorial Hospital Board and to be elected to the Lincoln Country Club Board.

"There have been a lot of people who have taken a chance on me through the years," Alice says. "Those are the people, plus my bank customers, that I thank for the opportunities I've had to succeed. They pushed me to achieve more than I thought I could at the time. They, along with my family, also taught the value of a hard-earned dollar."

It was those hard-earned dollars which Alice saved that established the $1 million Alice's Integrity* Loan Fund at the Lincoln Community Foundation. The micro-lending program's purpose is simple: provide support both financially and educationally to budding entrepreneurs and small business owners. It's the first program of its kind in Nebraska and has the power to change lives - one loan at a time.

"So many small businesses are at a disadvantage before they even get started," Alice says. "Banks typically can't make small, low interest loans without collateral. They especially don't encourage loans for entrepreneurs who have knicks on their credit score."

Alice's program is different. Every application receives attention and feedback. Those who provide a smart business plan, can prove their integrity is in line with Alice's vision, and have the gumption to work hard and run a small business will rise to the top of the applicants.

It's not a handout. Rather, it is a loan that recipients are expected to repay. The fund is set up to replenish itself year-after-year as loans are paid back, enabling more and more entrepreneurs to take advantage of this unique opportunity.

"This all started as an idea," shares Alice. "I knew I wanted to do something significant that allowed me to share the values I've learned with the next generation."

That is when Alice connected with the Lincoln Community Foundation.

"Alice came to us with a philanthropic vision," says Barbara Bartle, Lincoln Community Foundation president. "Our goal was to take her vision and make it as powerful for the community as it could be. We worked alongside Alice to find the right partners, craft the right plan and ultimately bring her vision to life."

Lincoln Community Foundation helped Alice shape her philanthropic goals by aligning her with Community Development Resources - a 501(c)(3) that provides financial services to small businesses and underserved markets not served by traditional financial institutions.

The partnership with Rick Wallace, executive director of Community Development Resources (CDR), will allow Alice to do more than just lend money to small business owners and entrepreneurs. It also allows her to provide valuable training and mentorship for each loan recipient. This training is being provided by Deb Payne, the CDR program manager of the Alice's Integrity Loan Fund. Payne has partnered with Nebraska Business Development Center (NBDC), SCORE, UNL and SCC to provide the technical assistance needed to grow and expand businesses.

And that is how the program got its name. *Alice's Integrity Loan Fund* intends to teach entrepreneurs self-discipline, social responsibility and, above all, it asks recipients to have integrity - the trait Alice both admires in and demands of those she works with in the business world.

"Flash and fancy have never been my favorite things," says Alice. "I believe that it was my prudent approach to spending less than I earned throughout my life that allowed me to create this program. This will be my greatest contribution to our community, and I can't wait to see what these loan recipients do with it."¤

*Integrity: "An uncompromising adherence to a code of moral, artistic or other values; utter sincerity, honesty and candor; avoidance of deception, expediency, artificiality or shallowness of any kind."
- WEBSTER'S THIRD INTERNATIONAL DICTIONARY

From AMERICAN BANKER magazine

Alice's
*Integrity*Loan Fund*

EXCERPT

Character is collateral: Even at age 86, Nebraska banking veteran Alice Dittman isn't done making loans. She put up $1 million of her own money to create a microlending program that emphasizes the character of applicants and doesn't require collateral.

Since the inception of Alice's Integrity Loan Fund, ...loans have been made... for enterprises like salons, a T-shirt printing shop, cleaning businesses and a grocery store. "I spent over 60 years working in banking and I am never tired of it," said Dittman. "This is probably the riskiest type of credit you can do. It is hard to make the overhead and hard to make a profit at 5.5% interest."

Her one disappointment with the initiative? IRS rules prevent her from getting directly involved in the loans and giving the entrepreneurs advice.

The Power Structure
Lincoln's Leaders— chosen by the leaders

LINCOLN JOURNAL-STAR AUGUST 13, 1995
THIS ARTWORK APPEARED IN AN
ARTICLE BY ANN HARRELL

► Here's how Lincoln's 10 most powerful people stack up: At the top, Lincoln Mayor Mike Johanns. Clockwise from Johanns: Jim Abel, Robert Duncan, D.B. "Woody" Varner, Orrin Wilson, Tom Osborne, James Stuart Jr., Duane Acklie, Alice Dittman, Gov. Ben Nelson.

Art/KIM STOLZER

Dittman prefers low profile as banker

By Gene Kelly

In national banking circles, Alice Dittman of Lincoln is regarded as a candid, articulate spokeswoman. Some consider her one of the most astute women bankers in America.

The past two years she has been a director of the American Bankers Association, the first Nebraskan to ever serve on that board.

In Lincoln, Mrs. Dittman, president of Cornhusker Bank, seems to prefer a low profile.

She takes quiet pride in having been the first female bank president in Lincoln, a post she assumed in 1975 after her father, G.A. Frampton, retired. It was the same year that her husband, Marcus, died.

Before the charter was moved to Lincoln, the Frampton family had owned the Farmers State Bank in Davey.

World of women

Although her banking career spans more than three decades, Mrs. Dittman continues to work hard to maintain her bank's growth record; since she became president, its assets have shown an average annual growth rate of 15 percent.

Cornhusker Bank had assets of almost $24 million on Dec. 31!

This suburban bank has been in its new building at 11th and Cornhusker Highway since September 1979.

Alice Dittman (right) says her staff, which includes Karen Edstrom, teller, (left) and Cheryl Socha, head teller, is largely responsible for the continuing growth of Cornhusker Bank in Lincoln.

...continued

Involved citizen

She takes pride in being an involved citizen.

But Mrs. Dittman is becoming much more vocal about an image problem she feels bankers have.

"Bankers have not told the banking story — what we do for the fees charged," she said. "We don't make a product; service is what we sell.

"When we ask customers why they bank with us, they tell us it's because they are comfortable here and feel they know our staff personally. Convenience, of course, is a big factor for some."

Banks are not nearly as profitable as the public might believe, she said. "A well-managed bank will net 1 percent on its total assets. The bigger the bank, the lower the margin."

Nebraska banks are more profitable than most, mainly because so many are small, she said. But many are being hit by increased loan losses.

The main reason that loan interest rates have not dropped in recent months, she said, is the fact that "bankers don't believe that inflation has been licked." Federal deficits are soaking up savings at such a fast pace, she said, that bankers feel "wild and fluctuating rates" may return.

Mrs. Dittman says all services offered by a bank "should stand on their own two feet." Why? "While a banker tends to think he makes his profit on interest income from loans, if he analyzes his bottom line, it will parallel his service charges."

"Too often these services are not properly priced, to pass the costs along to the customer. If you think about it, a checking account is a very valuable accounting service."

Testimony

A few days ago, Mrs. Dittman testified against LB95, a proposal that would prevent a bank or savings and loan from placing a service charge on a savings account.

"Nearly 35 percent of the savings accounts at Cornhusker Bank have balances of less than $100; yet the average annual cost to the bank of maintaining the account is $17.75. Is it right or fair to prevent us from levying a service charge?" she asked.

Although saying that the deregulation of interest rate ceilings has made banking "more exciting," Mrs. Dittman contends that even if banks and other financial institutions aren't competing on a level playing field, they should have to "use the same rule books, and change sides" periodically.

A Nebraska bank must have a capital-to-deposit ratio of 8 percent; a savings and loan must keep 2 percent in reserves. Money-market mutual funds have no reserve requirements.

"Thrift institutions are eager to convince the public that they are the same as a bank. Why? They want to identify with the stability that's associated with a banking charter," she said.

Examination procedures "should be comparable" among financial institutions, Mrs. Dittman said.

Smaller banks will survive

She is a firm believer that smaller banks will survive today's more intense financial-services competition. "There are predictions that the number of banks in America will shrink from 14,000 to about 8,500 by 1990. I don't believe it," she said.

"The small bank is often more efficient," she said.

"In the Midwest, we have a responsibility to keep banks safe and sound. At Cornhusker Bank, we want to make every credit-worthy loan, but not overloan; after all, the money still has to be paid back."

A key element in her bank's growth, she feels, is "little quality services" big banks usually don't offer.

"We stress verification of signatures and return processed checks to customers. Our staff would tend to catch a problem on an account sooner too," she said.

A drive-up automatic teller machine nicknamed "The Kernel," available to customers 24 hours a day, is a money-saver for the bank. "And I do love things that save money," she said.

Believes in education

Mrs. Dittman, 51, is a great believer in continuing education, especially in holding training sessions for her staff of 35. Adaptability is stressed. "An employee should consciously try to increase his productivity; I want every one to feel a personal responsibility for the bank, plus having a chance for personal growth."

In pursuit of her own education, Mrs. Dittman attended Radcliffe, the Graduate School of Banking at the University of Wisconsin, and received a bachelor's and master's degree from the University of Nebraska-Lincoln.

She is obviously proud of another success story — her role in raising three children as a single parent.

Dawn, who is a graduate of the University of Nebraska-Lincoln and has her master's from Northwestern, is on the staff of a Chicago advertising agency; John is a junior at UNL; and Doug is a freshman at the University of Kansas.

Kudos to Alice Dittman

OUR VIEW | LINCOLN JOURNAL-STAR AUGUST 6, 2011

Thanks to Alice Dittman for providing a welcome antidote for our nausea over the spectacle of firms deemed too big to fail.

The retired CEO of Cornhusker Bank is giving $1million over three years to establish a micro-lending program in Lincoln for people who want to start a business.

What a creative, fitting and enduring way for the pioneering banker to leave a mark.

Alice's Integrity Loan Fund at the Lincoln Community Foundation will offer 6 percent, unsecured three-year loans of no more than $5,000.

The program will be administered by Community Development Resources, which not only will help select loan recipients—there will be denials—but also provide mandatory coaching, training and mentoring.

To qualify, applicants must be a resident of Lancaster County, have a written business plan, documented qualifications, be willing to use the Nebraska Business Development Center and willing to accept mentoring from the Service Core of Retired Executives.

The loans might be used for buying a sewing machine, a computer for a home business or for expenses involved in setting up a housecleaning business, to cite a few possibilities.

The program emulates the micro-lending programs begun by Muhammad Yunus, the Bangladeshi economist who won a Nobel Peace Prize in 2006 for founding the Grameen Bank.

The bank founded by Yunus has spread rapidly across the globe because it filled a need and proved successful—all based on the concept that poor people will be just as financially responsible as the tycoons on Wall Street. Or perhaps more responsible, come to think of it.

Interestingly, one of the few branches of Grameen America is in Omaha. Dittman and Barb Bartle, president of the Lincoln Community Foundation, paid a fact-finding visit as part of developing Dittman's loan fund.

Dittman explained her motivation this way: "My career was made through people who took a chance on me at a time when women were not influential in business. There are plenty of great business plans with smart entrepreneurs that have been overlooked much like I could have been."

The history of philanthropy is replete with examples of successful business leaders who have created a legacy through donations that involved putting their names on buildings.

Nothing wrong with that.

But there's something special about a donation that strikes out in a new direction in the realm of charitable giving.

We hope that *Alice's Integrity Loan Fund* gives rise to thousands of individual success stories in coming years and that Dittman's legacy grows and grows. ¤

Nebraska native breaks 'glass ceiling' in banking

LINCOLN (AP) — Somewhere in Alice Dittman's files is the Wall Street Journal article that first coined the phrase "glass ceiling."

It seems fitting that the yellowed article sits somewhere in the files of this semi-retired banker; she's been quietly pushing that ceiling for years.

Alice Dittman, 71, cracked the glass ceiling by her actions, not by words, political stands or protests. She did it quietly, in part by necessity, certainly with a wealth of knowledge and a fervent enthusiasm for her profession.

Dittman, who was born in Havelock, may be good with numbers, but she is just as good with people, and that's the what drives her.

"What I like best is figuring out how to make a loan work for the customer and the bank," she said. "I feel that is the way I can be creative. You don't think of a bank as art, but if you can make things work for people it's an art form."

Her daughter, who became a bank vice president at the age of 30 and is now staying home to rear her son, said her mother is tough, resilient and focused. She said that, along with good common sense, is what makes her mom a success.

●

> *'She always told me,*
> *'Don't worry about*
> *something you can do*
> *nothing about, look*
> *for solutions."*
>
> **Dawn Dittman**
> About her mother

●

"My mother is an eternal optimist," Dawn Dittman Coronado said. "She always told me, 'Don't worry about something you can do nothing about, look for solutions.'"

That is why, 26 years ago, a newly widowed Dittman faced with the daunting prospect of rearing three children alone, returned to Lincoln from her home in Kansas City, Mo., and took over the reins of Cornhusker Bank from her father.

Just like that, a tall, lanky, outgoing Dittman became the first woman bank president in Lincoln or Omaha and one of only a handful around the country.

It is why, Dittman recently was given a Kiwanis Award for Distinguished Service, an award bestowed upon only four other women in its 79-year-history. Not that being the first woman to do something traditionally accomplished by men is particularly new to Dittman.

Consider Dittman's other "firsts": first chairwoman of the Bryan Memorial Hospital board; first chairwoman of the Lincoln Chamber of Commerce and the Nebraska State Chamber of Commerce; first woman president of the Nebraska Bankers Association; first chairwoman of the American Bankers Association Community Bankers Council; first woman to serve on the Lincoln Country Club board.

"I've been very, very fortunate," she said.

FREMONT TRIBUNE | OCTOBER 19, 2001

Alice Dittman is Panel Member

Alice Frampton Dittman, vice president of the Cornhusker Bank, will be in Cambridge Mass. Saturday to be a panel participant at the 25th anniversary of the Harvard-Radcliffe Program of Business Administration. The subject is "The Work-Oriented Life is the Interesting One." Mrs. Dittman, a NU graduate, was graduated in 1953 from the Harvard-Radcliffe Program of Business Administration—a one year graduate course for women.

LINCOLN JOURNAL-STAR MAY 8, 1963

George Andrew Frampton
1894 -1981

Cecile Meyer Frampton
1898 -1984

My father George Frampton bought the Farmers State Bank of Davey in 1949. In 1960 he moved the bank to Lincoln and renamed it Cornhusker Bank. Pictured is the Davey bank building as it looked in its early days.

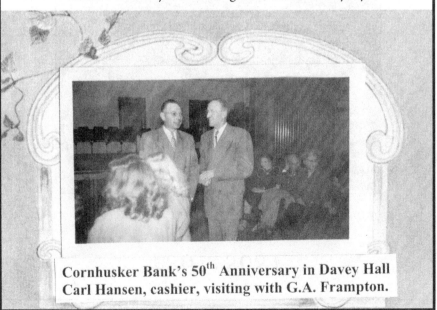

Cornhusker Bank's 50th Anniversary in Davey Hall Carl Hansen, cashier, visiting with G.A. Frampton.

Cornhusker Bank marks 100 years

In an age of national banking giants, the Lincoln bank has survived by giving customers what they want.

COURTESY PHOTO

The Cornhusker Bank began as Farmers State Bank in this building, which opened in Davey on Aug. 24, 1903.

LINCOLN JOURNAL-STAR AUGUST 24, 2003 | STORY BY ROOD CAYTON

A hundred years ago, banks served pretty much the same purpose they now serve, Cornhusker Bank chairman Alice Dittman says.

They were a safe place for the people of a community to put their money and a way for residents to reinvest in their village through loans to their neighbors.

So while the automobile was still a rich man's toy, manned flight was the domain of people named Wright, and Nebraska "foot-ball" coach Walter C. "Bummy" Booth was leading his team into a 10-0 season, Farmers State Bank (now Cornhusker Bank) was born in Davey. The bank's doors opened Aug. 24, 1903. The original charter hangs in the boardroom at Cornhusker Bank's headquarters.

The original 14 investors included several bankers with ties to other communities along with farmers, grocers and friends.

The first day's deposits totaled $12,000 — more than $240,000 in today's dollars.

Such a strong initial showing may help explain how the bank weathered the Great Depression without closing and emerged independent from a period that has seen banking go national and many smaller institutions gobbled up by out-of-state giants.

Other factors, Cornhusker Bank officials say, included a record matching larger institutions' conveniences, and a dedication to quality service.

Dittman's involvement with the bank began in 1949 when her father, G.A. Frampton, bought Farmers State Bank.

Dittman helped plan the 50th anniversary celebration. She talks of filing checks by the customer's name and noting the number of cows and bulls owned by a loan applicant.

Gone are the times when check payments were noted by written descriptions. A bank employee would, in indelible ink, take down information that's now recorded in less than a wink: the names of payor and payee, the check number, the amount....

Dittman said the fastest bank employees could record three checks a minute. Now, [2003] Cornhusker Bank uses a machine that can sort and photograph 600 checks a minute.

In between, Farmers State Bank moved to Lincoln and took its current name. Frampton said at the time, that the move was a response to increasing business in Lincoln and other parts of Lancaster County. He said a Lincoln location would be more central among the bank's customer base. ¤

Note: By the time this article was written in 2003, Cornhusker Bank had 112 employees and total assets of $231 million.

From $12,000 deposits in 1903
to $850,000,000 assets in 2021
by financing people's dreams

CORNHUSKER MAIN BANK 84th and O Street built in 2017

Cornhusker Bank's Assets Have Doubled Since Move

Cornhusker Bank total assets have doubled since Dec. 31, 1960 when the bank moved to its present location, 2834 No. 14th, stockholders w e r e told at their annual meeting Tuesday.

Total assets for 1964 were $2,057,761. Deposits increased about 10% in 1964 over the 1963 total and the number of customers increased by 12%.

Stock earnings of $5 per share were retained as additions to capital accounts and reserves.

Board directors re-elected were Norman Bulling, Alice Dittman, Cecile Frampton, G. A. Frampton, Robert E. Frampton, Forrest P. Hutson, A. Leicester Hyde Robert McGill, Kenneth H. Niedan, John W. Stewart and Karl A. Witt.

The board appointed the following officers: G. A. Frampton, chairman of the board and president; Kenneth H. Niedan, vice president and cashier; Alice Dittman and Cecile Frampton, vice presidents; Loren E. Babcock and James A. Mastera, assistant cashiers.

Cornhusker Bank on
North 14th Street

Lincoln Journal-Star
January 13, 1965

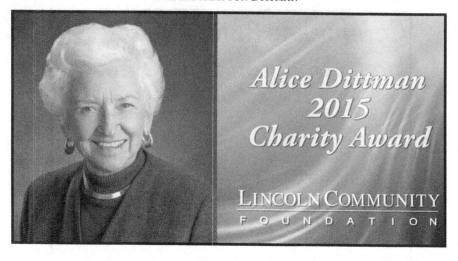

Lincoln Community Foundation
2015 Charity Award
{PENNY COSTELLO, VIDEO PRODUCTION/NARRATION}

NARRATOR: For Alice Dittman, banking was her heritage. It was in her blood. At a very early age, she learned the critical role that bankers and business play in any community.

Her early immersion in the business cultivated not only a sharp business acumen, but also an appreciation for the very human side of banking.

BARRY LOCKARD: ...Alice has always said things fade and rust, but the real value is in the relationships with people.

JIM MASTERA: What was one of her quotes...hm, "We get to finance peoples' dreams." And that is just a marvelous quote when you really put that into play. I just love that one.

TERESA ELLIOT: Once you get to know Alice on a more personal level you realize that, while she is very business focused, she has such a

caring heart that you can't help but fall in love with her.

NARRATOR: Alice began her career in the family business at Farmer's State Bank in Davey. She worked there while pursuing a business degree at UNL. At the time, in the early 1950's, only 10% of business majors were women. There she continued to break ground for countless women who would make the business world their own.

ROSS HECHT: Women's opportunities have been expanded greatly because of Alice Dittman. When you see what she has been able to do...and I hope that other women are encouraged by what she's been able to do...that that would be a real feather in her hat.

TERESA ELLIOT: Alice is a great person to make you believe in yourself. She helps you draw out strengths in yourself that sometimes I don't think you might know you had otherwise.

ALICE DITTMAN: I've been supportive in hiring two women for one job. I mean, nobody did that. And why did you have to have everybody come to work at eight o'clock and quit at five. It makes no sense. But I think that was a strength that we've shown, and still do.

I did have one bank president tell me that he would really like to have a woman on his bank board, but 'Alice? There just aren't any.'

And...I must admit, I didn't say much in response, because I thought 'there certainly are about half of your depositors who are female'.

NARRATOR: Through three generations, modest little Farmers' State Bank in Davey grew into Cornhusker Bank of Lincoln, with six branches and nearly half a billion dollars in assets. And much of that due to Alice's leadership and vision.

ROSS HECHT: She's a real forward thinker. She kind of sees out into the future and sees what's possible and what's not so possible and then she takes after it. She goes for it.

JIM MASTERA: She doesn't fail. And many times she'd say, "Jim, we have Plan One, but we also need Plan Two. You don't fail if you plan appropriately and you know where you're going."

NARRATOR: Since she took the helm at Cornhusker Bank in 1975, Alice Dittman is credited with several "firsts". She was the first woman to lead the Nebraska Bankers Association, the Lincoln Chamber of Commerce, the Nebraska Chamber of Commerce, and the Community Bankers Association—a division of the American Bankers Association.

JIM MASTERA: Much stronger than that was her contribution of time, and talent, and effort throughout the community, and throughout the banking industry, for that matter.

NARRATOR: John Guenzel met Alice when she agreed to serve on the board of First Nebraska Trust Company.

JOHN GUENZEL: We were a startup, beginning-from-scratch company, with no clients and nothing but good intentions and a plan to work. And Alice took a chance on us. She set an example and tone for our company. She is a true leader, and she helped at the staff level show and empower the people who work here what they could accomplish if they just performed at their best level.

NARRATOR: Ross Hecht had been friends with Alice since college. But when she came to him with a proposition to build housing for low-income elderly, she got right down to business.

ROSS HECHT: And she said, "Ross, this is a win-win situation. You don't have to think very long about it. I've got the papers here, why don't we just sign the papers and get on with it?" And I said, "Uh, okay." And I thought to myself 'She could sell ice to the Eskimos'. And so I signed the papers! It was a really good project for the city, for the community, for the elderly.

NARRATOR: She supported the Leaders Are Readers initiative aimed at elementary students. She sponsors the All-College Business Plan competition at UNL, and she continues to mentor small business owners. Her commitment to entrepreneurship and personal development are unsurpassed.

JIM MASTERA: For Alice, success isn't just measured by dollars. It's 'are you giving and contributing back to the community that you grew up in, that you live in, that you thrive in?'

ROSS HECHT: Whatever she is involved in, people recognize her talents and they want her to get more involved, and I think that's a real tribute to her abilities and her background.

ALICE: There's a flip side to it that you feel an even greater responsibility to live up to that recognition. I mean, you wouldn't want to let them down.

NARRATOR: To describe Alice Dittman in a few words, she's down-to-earth, generous, forward-thinking, but behind all that is a love of healthy competition.

JIM MASTERA: I think everyone knows about Alice playing tennis, and Alice playing golf. But not everyone knows about Alice playing pingpong. Alice refuses to get beat at the pingpong table and she rarely, rarely does.

ROSS HECHT: Do not play pingpong against her, especially for money.

NARRATOR: So what is a fitting legacy for someone so instrumental in Lincoln's growth and quality of life? For Alice Dittman, it's the micro-lending program *Alice's Integrity Loan Fund* that she established with one million dollars of her own resources.

ALICE: It's based on giving back, something that I know about and take the greatest joy in. And I can't tell you how much I hope people—women, primarily—but men and women will take advantage of this, so I want to see two hundred loans out there. I've created a profit center for two hundred people and then carrying on from there as those funds recycle.

ROSS HECHT: (chuckling) Well, that would be Alice, because she saw a need, for people that needed maybe just enough to get a little kick... (gesturing upward).

JIM MASTERA: It's serving everyone. And it helps our community. It builds economic strength, which is always one of Alice's concerns that something be financially stable and sound. Alice is so deserving of this award [Lincoln Community Foundation's 2015 Charity Award], because this lady is more than one person. Her own self is so widespread, and it is the fabric that continues to build Lincoln, Nebraska to be the community it has. And Alice rewards the community both through her involvement and through her financial commitment. So I can think of no better recipient for that award than Alice Dittman.

ALICE: As I've moved through life, you know, I've certainly had opportunities—certainly some more deserved than others—but I have said "Yes" at the right time to opportunities that come along. And hopefully I've enjoyed almost all of the stumbling blocks and built some stepping stones. ¤

Over the years I've taken great enjoyment in wearing the golden ear of corn that was given to me by the American Bankers Association. Below, it was a thrill to experience Ak-Sar-Ben with my children, daughters-in-law, brother Robert and his wife Eloise, in 2009.

Dollars and cents of LPS figures

75 percent of $408.9 million for recommended school improvements can be paid for without tax levy increase.

BY MARGARET REIST Nov. 6, 2005
Lincoln Journal Star

For Alice Dittman, the bottom line for just about everything she does is the price tag.

So when Dittman, chairman of the board for Cornhusker Bank, worked on a task force considering Lincoln Public Schools' building needs for the next decade, cost was a vital component.

"I don't tend to be able to come up with an answer without a price tag attached to it," she said. "I've always governed my own life like that. If I can't afford it, I won't buy it. I think schools should do the same."

That's why, when the task force finance committee looked at the dollars and cents of their recommendations, Dittman applauded.

She actually put her hands together and clapped.

She did it, she said, because what she heard was good news.

The numbers LPS officials provided the task force showed that more than three-quarters of the $408.9 million needed to implement all the recommended improvements could be paid for without raising the tax levy of $1.31 per $100 valuation.

"That's truly amazing," Dittman said. "I feel like it's doable, and I feel like the expertise that's gone into the numbers is sound."

For one thing, said Dittman—who spent her career shopping the bond market and handling her bank's portfolio — the estimates are not based on future growth, but on today's property valuations.

If you go

The task force that has been considering Lincoln Public Schools' building needs for the next 10 years will present its findings to the Lincoln Board of Education at 4:30 Tuesday at LPS District Offices, 5901 O St.

Banker gets Rotary club's annual honor

Cornhusker Bank President Alice M. Dittman has been named 1994 Nebraskan of the Year by the Downtown Lincoln Rotary Club.

Alice Dittman

The seventh annual award will be presented at a Tuesday luncheon in the Cornhusker Hotel ballroom.

Dittman, who became president of the bank in 1975, is president of the Nebraska Bankers Association and past chairwoman of both the Nebraska State Chamber of Commerce and the Lincoln Chamber of Commerce.

Criteria for the award include honesty, integrity and concern for others, service in charitable and civic causes and leadership and accomplishment in a field of employment. Dittman is the first woman to receive the honor.

Dittman is a past board member of the American Bankers Association and was named Phi Chi Theta Businesswoman of the Year in 1987. Other honors include being named the U.S. Small Business Administration Women in Business Advocate and winning the Distinguished Service Award from the Nebraska National Guard, both in 1989.

Dittman is a member of the University of Nebraska President's Advisory Committee and chairwoman of the finance committee for St. Paul United Methodist Church. She has served on the boards of Nebraska Wesleyan University and the Nebraska Independent College Foundation and is a past chairwoman of the Bryan Memorial Hospital board.

LINCOLN JOURNAL-STAR - JANUARY 10, 1994

Alice Dittman receives community builder award

Honor recognizes the board chairman for Cornhusker Bank as an involved member of the community.

Alice Dittman, chairman of the board for Cornhusker Bank, received the 2004 Roger T. Larson Community Builder Award at the Greater Lincoln Chamber Foundation Gala Friday evening at the Embassy Suites Hotel.

The award recognizes a community member for involvement, volunteerism and a successful business career that has proved instrumental in the growth of Lincoln.

Dittman was the first female bank president in Lincoln or Omaha and was the first female chair of the Lincoln Chamber of Commerce. She was also the first woman to chair the Nebraska Chamber of Commerce of Industry, the Bryan Memorial Hospital board, and the first woman named president of the Nebraska Bankers Association.

DITTMAN

"Alice has been an integral part of the Lincoln community for over 30 years," according to Jim Fram, president of the chamber. "Her contributions have had a lasting and meaningful impact in the continued growth of Lincoln."

Past winners of the award include Roger T. Larson, for whom the award is named, 2001; Helen Boosalis, 2002; and Lew Harris, 2003.

Burnham Yates Award:
Alice Dittman-Cornhusker Bank

Alice Dittman has been a pioneer in the Lincoln banking community. Alice started her career 50 years ago as a cashier in her father's bank, succeeding him as President & CEO in 1975. Alice has been a pillar in the community with the belief that to be successful in business, you have to give back to the community. This is evidenced in her numerous leadership positions benefiting the community of Lincoln.

UNIVERSITY OF NEBRASKA SCHOOL OF BUSINESS ADMINISTRATION

Q & A with Alice Dittman

NOVEMBER 12, 2018

ALICE DITTMAN ACHIEVED MANY FIRSTS DURING HER CAREER
INCLUDING BEING NAMED THE FIRST WOMAN TO BECOME A
BANK PRESIDENT IN LINCOLN AND OMAHA.

CLASS OF 1952 & 1955

A pioneer in business in Nebraska, Alice Dittman achieved many firsts including being named the first woman to become a bank president in Lincoln and Omaha. When she took over as president and CEO of Cornhusker Bank in 1975, the value of the bank was $8 million and she grew it to nearly $236 million. She became the first woman to chair the Bryan Hospital Board of Directors in 1982, the Lincoln Chamber of Commerce in 1988, the Nebraska Chamber of Commerce in 1992 and the Community Bankers Council in 1997. She also was the first woman to become president of the Nebraska Bankers Association in 1993.

Share your advice from your experiences being the first.

I never thought about being first, I just did it. I always did my homework and arrived prepared. I'm all about banking and I'd spend an hour before bed reading things I didn't have time to read at work. A strong work ethic is part of anyone's success.

I'm a big fan of the University of Nebraska. Gaining confidence is having a background and working hard. I earned my master's degree because I knew management would make small banks more successful and better than everyone else, as not many men in banking had an advanced degree.

What is the secret to success?

I was introduced to Warren Buffett (the Oracle of Omaha and a 1951 graduate of the College of Business) at a wedding in Omaha. He said, "Are you the banker?" and I said, "Are you the financier?" My response was a bit flippant, but we all laughed and I do think it might be a secret of success in not taking yourself too seriously. It always felt good to make people laugh about something.

The easiest way to get to know people is to talk to them. I'd walk into a room full of men and make a circle around the room. I'd say, "Hi," and put my hand out. In 1975, people didn't know to put their hands out, and I'd leave it there to shake. It's important to include others. Nod or smile – those are easy to give away and important in comfort building.

What is the scariest thing you have done?

It is not easy to go in places where you may or may not feel welcome. Just think about that, if you are the minority, how does that impact you? Would you leave or hang around and try to learn something? We need more minorities in our population to bring a new dimension to Lincoln.

The scariest thing now is the lack of congeniality in our nationwide system of checks and balances. Not getting things accomplished because there is no give and take. You have to give. That part seems to be lacking. In any organization, the members have to agree and get along to get anything done. Democrat Bob Kerrey and Republican Chuck Hagel (who recently spoke at the university together) talk to each other. They want the best for our country. ¤

Here my brother Bob (in the center) joined us for the ribbon-cutting ceremony at the Bethany branch.

Nebraska bankers name Dittman 1st female leader

JOHN BARRETTE, LINCOLN JOURNAL, APRIL 29, 1993

Alice M. Dittman, who becomes the first woman to head the Nebraska Bankers Association beginning Friday, offered praise and criticism for President Clinton today.

Dittman, the chairman, president and chief executive officer of the Cornhusker Bank in Lincoln, gave the kudos for work on red tape and the criticism for the administration's spending-budget cutting approach.

"We feel like he understands our problems," she said, speaking of Clinton's efforts to cut through red tape for bankers so lending can help move the economy forward.

[She] offered this mild criticism of Clinton's budget work:

"Bankers probably tend to think in terms of net debt reduction rather than spending first and reductions later."

...Dittman's main remarks in a pre-installation interview focused on Nebraska's home town banks, the pride of the bankers that run them and the relationship fostered between local businesses, depositors and the bankers.

"We're the engine that drives the local economies," she said. "It takes the home town bank to provide the multiplier effect within the community. You can't get that impact from any other deposit-gathering source."

She said the multiplier effect means dollars put to work at home roll over six times in the local economy.

Dittman, who started as a cashier at the Farmers State Bank in Davey, has been in banking more than 40 years.

Her priorities as president of the NBA will be persuading Congress to cut red tape, which she says costs depositors as well as bankers, and taking her message about banks' roles in communities to the public.

Her view of being the first woman to head the NBA: "It's only been 103 years. I guess I'm here at the right time." ¤

Rotary Club names Alice Dittman
its 1994 Nebraskan of the Year

LINCOLN JOURNAL, JANUARY 15, 1994

Alice M. Dittman...was named 1994 Nebraskan of the Year by the Downtown Lincoln Rotary Club.

The first female recipient of the honor, Dittman accepted the award during a luncheon in the Cornhusker Hotel ballroom.

Dittman is president of the Nebraska Bankers Association and a past chairman of both the Nebraska State Chamber of Commerce and the Lincoln Chamber of Commerce.

She was the first woman elected to all three of those positions. ¤

Arthritis Foundation honors bank leader

LINCOLN JOURNAL, MAY 23, 1993

Alice M. Dittman has been chosen as the Arthritis Foundation's 1993 Woman of the Year.

Dittman, president and chief executive officer of Cornhusker Bank, will be honored at the 16th Annual Arthritis Foundation Woman of the Year Gala and Silent Auction November 21at the Cornhusker Convention Center.

Dittman's professional affiliations include chairman of the Nebraska State Chamber of Commerce, president-elect of the Nebraska Bankers Association, past president of the Nebraska Electronic Transfer System, past board member of the American Bankers Association and past board member of People's Natural Gas.

Her past community activities include serving on the Nebraska Wesleyan University Board of Governors, chairman of the Bryan Memorial Hospital board of trustees, board member of the Nebraska Independent College Foundation, and chairman of the Lincoln Chamber of Commerce board.

Dittman is currently on the president's advisory committee for the University of Nebraska. She also is involved with St. Paul United Methodist Church and P.E.O. and is the first female member of the Country Club of Lincoln board of directors.

She has received other honors including Phi Chi Theta's business woman of the year, the Lincoln Jaycees CEO Award, the Lincoln Independent Business Association's Business of the Year Award, and numerous other distinguished service and alumni awards.

Proceeds from the gala will benefit the Nebraska Chapter of the Arthritis Foundation. ¤

WOMEN IN *Philanthropy*

November 1, 2005

Alice M. Dittman earns United Way's "FOUNDERS AWARD"

Approximately 125 local men and women gathered September 21st for the sixth annual United Way of Lincoln and Lancaster County "Women in Philanthropy" luncheon. The goal of the event is to publicly recognize the impact women have on both the economic viability and quality of life in our community.

Alice Dittman was the featured speaker and recipient of the second annual United Way "Founder's Award". Founders of this group created in 1999 include Kim Robak, Linda Robinson Rutz, Barbara Tolliver Haskins, Kathy Campbell, and Nancy Fuchs.   -STORY BY GAIL STOKLASA

BUSINESS

Theories differ on lack of women on business boards

Women on Lincoln business boards aren't as rare as the occasional super-heroine in pop culture's past, but neither are they as plentiful as female power figures on today's television shows.

For every Wonder Woman there were scads of mythical macho men to role model for boys, such as Batman, Superman, or the Lone Ranger.

The Wonder Women of the board room are emerging, but Lincoln business leaders acknowledge it could take up to a decade or more before boardrooms reflect a good measure of the pop culture revolution under way on TV screens.

Lincoln business leaders say board rooms will change as years pass and female midmanagement executives rise to the top, ascending to boards as well. Some say that is coming quickly.

JOHN BARRETTE
SUNDAY JOURNAL-STAR JULY 9, 1989

Now, however, Alice Dittman's name constantly crops up when businessmen talk about the few females who head businesses or are in top management posts and so are asked to serve on boards.

Under Dittman's leadership, Cornhusker Bank has grown to assets of $61 million from $8.5 million in 1975.

The president and chief executive officer of that growing bank is one of three females on its board. She believes men or women who serve on business boards need a solid foundation, but that doesn't confine her board to upper-management colleagues.

END OF ARTICLE EXCERPT

"It's not a complicated business," she says, "and it shouldn't be. I have a balance sheet and a profit-and-loss statement every day. Together, that's a steering tool that makes banking an easy ship to steer. But it turns like a tanker, not like a speedboat."

"I think it's an irreversible change."

— Alice Dittman,
president and CEO of Cornhusker State Bank
and first woman to chair traditionally male-led Lincoln Chamber of Commerce

Old-boy, old-style networking is gradually being chipped away by integrated organizations where men — and women — are working together.

Story by C.J. Schepers

Old boys' club no longer that

INSIDE LINCOLN BUSINESS | OCTOBER 1, 1990

EXCERPT

Chisel, chisel, chisel. Believe it or not, old-boy, old-style networking is gradually being chipped away by integrated organizations where men— and women—are working together. The infiltration has been slow. But a mixture is developing.

...Alice Dittman, president and CEO of Cornhusker State Bank, was the first woman to chair the traditionally male-led Lincoln Chamber of Commerce.

"I think it's an irreversible change," she said.

Dittman is on the board of directors of Leadership Lincoln, a personal development group now in its sixth year.

Leadership Lincoln has a well-balanced mixture of men and women working—and leading—together.

"I think Leadership Lincoln is probably the best example of new networking," Dittman said.

...Dittman said she also feels it is good to have both mixed and separate organizations, depending on the purpose.

"I purposely keep in touch with some women's organizations because I want to know what they're thinking," she said.

Dittman, who herself is an influential business leader, said that she has seen networking changes for women in business, but not much in the areas of camaraderie and personal investments. Typically, men are still the first ones to benefit from that type of networking through business organizations.

"It's changed less in the business world than it has in the volunteer sector," she said.

Dittman said there are not as many women achieving CEO levels as there should be, partly because networking "takes more than one generation to get the building blocks in place."

"I do hope more men and women in leadership roles will take one younger individual to mentor," she said. ¤

Alice Dittman Talking Points
NEBRASKA BANKERS ASSOCIATION SPEECH
SEPTEMBER 2012

★ Bankers are dedicated to your success. You see us as community lenders. We also are committed to our role as community leaders.

★ Bankers are dedicated to serving our customers -- making your dreams come true, creating jobs, and growing our communities and our economy. That's why we're bankers.

★ I like being a banker. But bankers are facing a challenging environment. It's difficult to be a banker in today's world.

★ There are 7300 banks in the U.S. – about half as many as there were 20 years ago.

★ The good news first – in one sense, things are looking better for our banks.

··· Today's banks hold $13 trillion in assets and employ 2 million people.

··· At the end of the first quarter of the year, the FDIC -- the Federal Deposit Insurance Corp., which is funded by the banks, not the taxpayers, the banks -- reported that 97% of the industry was well-capitalized.

··· Business lending is increasing.

··· Loan quality continues to improve.

··· Deposits have increased.

··· And bank earnings are getting better.

★ A strong, growing and profitable banking sector is critical to our communities – and to the nation's economic vitality. Steady improvements in asset quality and earnings form a strong base that can propel lending to businesses and consumers.

★ More good news – you've all heard of TARP, the government program that was created to curb the financial crisis of 2007-2008.

★ I am pleased to report that TARP has resulted in a positive return to taxpayers.

★ Today, banks have done the right and responsible thing, paying back — with interest — money invested in them during the financial crisis by the federal government.

★ As a result, TARP's bank programs — often misperceived as causing losses — have provided a significant return to taxpayers.

★ The government invested $245 billion into TARP bank programs, a small portion (35 percent) of the $700 billion that was authorized.

★ Banks have repaid $266 billion through principal and interest payments — representing a $21 billion positive return to taxpayers so far.

★ The U.S. Treasury Department estimates that TARP's bank programs ultimately will provide a profit to the taxpayer of more than $22 billion. That doesn't appear to be a story that our news media wants to cover!

★ But there is another side to the story, one that bankers like me find very frightening.

★ Banking is a heavily regulated industry — more so now than ever. We are, after all, the guardians of your money, the custodian of so many hopes and dreams. But when regulation becomes a burden to the engine that fuels economic growth, it becomes a burden to the economy itself.

★ When the regulatory pendulum swings too far, as we've seen recently, it gets in the way of our efforts to promote economic recovery and job creation. That's what's happening now. And that's a problem for all of us.

★ Banks devote substantial time and effort to regulatory compliance. That compliance burden – ensuring that every regulation, rule, and guideline is followed – hits smaller banks especially hard. Bankers are working to help find some balance, to enable banks to better serve their customers and communities.

★ Has anyone recently completed a home loan? You know the paperwork that you now get to complete. I would hate to think about the amount of time it would take a customer to read every document that we now have to put in front of you, let alone understand what it all says.

★ All of that paperwork is mandated for the sake of consumer protection.

★ I'm not sure how well it is working for banks -- or our customers.

★ In an effort to encourage complete disclosure and consumer awareness, Congress has created a bureaucracy of paperwork that totally misses the objective.

★ Banking relationships are built on trust, not on 100 or more pages of documentation and disclosures that very few people read or have a chance of understanding.

★ Two years ago – on July 21, 2010 -- President Obama signed into law the Dodd-Frank Wall Street Reform and Consumer Protection Act. At the time, Senator Chris Dodd of Connecticut headed the Senate Banking Committee, and Congressman Barney Frank of Massachusetts chaired the House Financial Services Committee.

★ That law, in particular . . .

   ... Impairs community banks' ability to serve our customers and communities.

   ... It impairs our ability to help you make your dreams come true.

   ... And it impairs our ability to help grow our communities and create jobs. Maybe that's why the unemployment rate is still more than 8.0%.

★ The Dodd-Frank Act was the result of a housing market gone crazy. It was also the result of excesses by Wall Street investment bankers and so-called mortgage bankers. So, when every sin of omission and commission was reported in the media, the report came out as "banks did this wrong and banks did that wrong." Most of us, the traditional banks, were painted with a very broad brush. Most of us were not responsible for the excesses.

★ Now we live with the consequences – the Dodd-Frank Act.

★ The result is estimated to be more than 5,000 pages of new regulations on traditional banks and years of uncertainty as to what the massive new rules will mean.

★ Much of Dodd Frank was designed to get at the very large investment banks and the mortgage "bankers."

★ I'm not even sure why they keep referring to Wall Street Investment Banks as "banks." They have no resemblance to the banks that you deal with in your personal and professional lives.

★ However, as we are finding out very quickly, regulation, like water, rolls downstream and community banks — smaller banks closest to their community — are getting crushed by these new rules and regulations.

★ Fewer than 30 percent of the regulations from Dodd-Frank have been "finalized."

★ For the median-sized bank — with only 37 employees — this regulatory burden is overwhelming.

★ The weight of these new rules creates pressure to hire additional compliance staff instead of loan officers.

★ It means more money spent on compliance, reducing resources that could be directly applied to serving a bank's customers and community. In the end, it means fewer loans are made, fewer jobs are created, and more costs are being incurred by banks and their customers.

★ So, what does that mean? Just look around. It means what we now have . . . real gross domestic product -- the output of goods and services produced by labor and property in the United States -- increased at an annual rate of just under 2 percent in the first quarter of 2012.

★ There's more to the consequences of the Dodd-Frank. Its regulations literally threaten the very survival of many community banks — and the towns they serve.

★ These banks had nothing to do with what happened to the economy in 2008. Yet, they are being crippled as the result of the pile-ons of regulations and costs. Either they'll find a buyer, or they'll get out of the business.

★ There is a danger that the Dodd-Frank regulations can hurt or destroy some small-bank business models. They just can't afford the added costs of compliance — and the reduced opportunity to invest in their community.

★ Bankers like me are working to tell the public, the press, and our elected officials that there is a problem here.

★ We all need to recognize that there will be reactions to the regulations that Dodd-Frank demands. We're working to make sure as an industry that those reactions are sensible and beneficial to the public, and not just crippling to an industry that's all about growth, prosperity and jobs.

★ We will work hard to pull ourselves out of the quicksand of new regulation, while at the same time working with Congress and the federal regulators to find more realistic solutions.

★ There are any number of other challenges that face our banks. I'll mention two – keeping up with technology, and its thieves, and competition that has been given an advantage we lack.

FIRST—TECHNOLOGY.

★ Banks and all of you in your businesses are dealing with new technologies. Our customers are dramatically changing the way they bank and do business.

★ Think about the ways that you can bank today:

- ⋯ Internet banking
- ⋯ Phone banking
- ⋯ Mobile banking
- ⋯ Bill payments
- ⋯ Treasury management services
- ⋯ And more.

★ We are working hard to accommodate all of our customers from every generation, but at the same time we want to make sure any changes we make or products that we add are offered and used in a safe and sound manner.

★ However, even as we add more and more technology options, we also continue to provide the branch and personal options that many of our customers still prefer in addition to the technology systems.

★ At the same time, hackers and crooks are growing in numbers. The banking industry, like each of us as consumers, has to be cautious in how we handle our banking business, our computers, and our passwords.

NOW LET ME MENTION ONE MORE CHALLENGE TO BANKING.

★ Banks, especially community banks, are also challenged by unfair competition. There is a Senate bill that would allow a handful of very large credit unions to double their business lending. Banks are opposed to this for several reasons.

★ Credit unions' shared mission is to serve people of modest means. Most of them have stuck to that mission. However, there are a growing group of extremely large credit unions that have essentially become very "bank like" and now want to jump knee deep into business lending.

★ What's wrong with competition? Nothing at all — when it's fair and on a level playing field.

★ You may not know it, but credit unions pay no federal income taxes. None at all. Anybody here like that? Anybody have a for-profit business that does not pay taxes on its net profits?

★ Credit unions originally received this federal tax exemption to facilitate their mission. As some of them have varied far off path from this mission, our view is that the tax exemption should also go away.

★ Wouldn't it be great for all of us if gross income equaled net income, or gross wages equaled take home pay?

★ The estimated loss of federal tax revenues from these large credit unions increasing their business lending is projected to be north of $354 million over 10 years. Is that fiscally responsible? Somebody still has to pay for border security, national defense and Medicare and Medicaid.

> What was the old saying? "Don't tax him, don't tax me, tax that fellow behind the tree?" I'll bet every business and every profession you represent is taxed. We're the ones behind the tree.

★ If credit unions want to offer business loans and all bank services, they should become taxpaying banks. That conversion process to a mutual savings bank is available to them. (And the NBA would then welcome them as members!)

★ Community banks also face major competition in the ag lending area from the Farm Credit System, another tax-advantaged government-sponsored enterprise that is similar to Fannie Mae and Freddie Mac. Unlike Fannie and Freddie, the Farm Credit System is the only government-sponsored enterprise with retail lending authority. It was originally charged with serving farmers and ranchers who could not otherwise obtain credit. Today the Farm Credit System, similar to bank-like credit unions, strives to maintain its advantaged status while pushing the boundaries prescribed by its original mission.

★ Congress should not continue to try to pick winners and losers through tax code advantages. Even the playing field and let the best competitors thrive.

★ I've covered a lot of ground with you today. We've examined the trends and spotlighted the challenges. The big item for me is:

··· When it comes to regulation and the banks' regulatory burden, the pendulum has swung too far. This is especially true for community banks that really had nothing to do with the problems that were created.

··· When you burden any business with too many regulations and too much government bureaucracy, it impedes business and profits, which negatively impacts growth in revenue and growth in jobs.

··· It's at odds with the ability of banks to make the loans that build small businesses and communities, and drive the economic recovery.

··· A world without regulation is not the answer. That would also lead to bad outcomes.

··· What is needed is a better balance. I'm sure many of you that run businesses feel the same about many of your new regulations and requirements.

★ Let me go back to where I began.

★ Growing and progressive communities need growing, progressive and strong banks. Growing and progressive banks also need growing, progressive and strong communities.

★ Yes, we really are in this . . . together. ¤

"Banking relationships are built on trust, not on 100 or more pages of documentation and disclosures that very few people read or have a chance of understanding."

-ALICE DITTMAN

NET...NEBRASKA PATHBREAKERS

TRANSCRIPTION OF NET VIDEO — PENNY COSTELLO, PRODUCER/NARRATOR

"ALICE HAS THRIVED ON THE ROAD LESS TRAVELED."

ON NEBRASKA PATHBREAKERS, WOMEN WHOSE COURAGE AND TENACITY HAVE BROKEN BOUNDARIES AND MOVED THE NEEDLE ON CHANGE.

NARRATOR: When she became president of Nebraska Cornhusker Bank in 1975, Alice Dittman made a radical break from the traditional role of wife and mother to boldly enter a realm dominated by men.

Alice Dittman smashes barriers. In 1975 she stepped into a man's world when she became president of Cornhusker Bank in Lincoln—the first woman to do so in Lincoln and Omaha. She made it work.

More recently, Alice was diagnosed with jaw cancer, but to know Alice, nothing seems to stop her. Not even cancer.

Born to a banker father and a college-educated mother, Alice's story began October 1st, 1930.

ALICE: One of my bad memories when I misbehaved was my first day of school. And my mother walked me to Randolph Elementary. It was just a half-day Kindergarten. Later I met my mother coming to walk me back home. Well, I was a big girl now and I wouldn't walk with her. She just laughed about it and walked behind me.

Well, I was always thrifty, and my dad let me count the money in his billfold.

And that was good experience, you know. I don't know why I wanted to count it, but I did, so maybe it's in my genes a little bit. And being thrifty. But things like that were fun. It was a great way to grow up.

NARRATOR: As both of her parents had a post-secondary education, it was only expected that Alice would attend college. In 1952 she graduated from the University of Nebraska at Lincoln with a degree in Business.

ALICE: I wouldn't have had the opportunities I had if I hadn't been a pretty good student. That's probably one of the reasons why I got the chance to go back East for a postgraduate year.

NARRATOR: In 1952, the doors to Harvard Graduate School of Business were closed to women. So Alice enrolled at Radcliffe, a women's college in Cambridge, Massachusetts, and was taught by Harvard Business professors.

ALICE: And it was Harvard's excuse for not admitting women to their business school. I had a great year, and I had the opportunity to learn a great deal being with girls that were top students. You know...I mean, it was just an experience I couldn't have had in Nebraska at that time.

NARRATOR: With her postgraduate year behind her, Alice was back in Nebraska working at the family bank. She married Mark Dittman in 1955. One year later she earned a Masters' in Finance and Management at UNL, a degree not many men had at the time. Alice continued working until she had her first child in 1959. Then she did what women at the time did: she became a stay-at-home mom.

DOUG DITTMAN: I wouldn't have wanted to be raised by anyone else, you know? I'm really proud of Mom. She's really done well.

NARRATOR: Doug Dittman is the youngest of Alice's three children. He owns a restaurant in Lincoln, and lives on a farm that once belonged to his grandfather.

DOUG DITTMAN: It was fun. Mom and Dad had lots of friends and it was the 60s and early 70s and ... people would sit around ... talking about whatever.

ALICE: Mark died in 1975. He died of cancer. But you didn't think about it being hard. You just did it.

DOUG DITTMAN: I know that as kids we never missed a beat. We had a little powwow about 'what are we going to do'.

ALICE: And my kids were 11, 13, and 15. But I think it may have made my kids a little more mature... You take things in steps, you know? It's amazing what you can accomplish.

NARRATOR: Another big change

came three months later, in July, when Alice's father retired as president of Cornhusker Bank. When Alice assumed the helm at age 45, she became the first woman to be president of a bank in Lincoln and Omaha.

ANNE BURKHOLDER: She has always been a very, very strong woman, and someone who is very focused, but somebody also with a very big heart, and you look at her kids and you know that she did a great job with them.

NARRATOR: In 1987, Anne Burkholder had already been turned down by other banks when she asked Alice for a business loan. A painter, Anne wanted to create a collaborative space where artists could live, work, and display their art. Today it's known as the Burkholder Project.

ANNE BURKHOLDER: The word got out that I was looking for a building, and this is kind of interesting because Alice Dittman called me one day and said, "I have a building down here you need to look at." And she said, "Let's go have lunch." Alice is one of those people who are always looking out for the other person. I mean, here she is, she's a conservative banker, but she's got a really big heart, and helping other people, I think, is one of the major things that she does.

DOUG DITTMAN: She's mentored so many. As a boy on, I remember a steady stream of usually single women that would come to the house, and either they were divorced or the husband died, and they asked, "What am I going to do?" because the women didn't know the finances.

ALICE: It's an important part of our bank: trying to get people *out* of debt and not keep them *in* debt.

NARRATOR: As president of Cornhusker Bank, Alice led the pack in adopting new electronic banking technology. She started a job-sharing program to help working mothers. She expanded bank assets from 8 million dollars to 235 million dollars. While running the bank and being a single parent, Alice accepted leadership roles in other organizations, and continues to be active in the Lincoln community.

DOUG DITTMAN: She was just so darn capable, you know? She was always the smartest person in the room and the most capable person in the room. And, I think, you know, she could be very mannish, which she probably had to be in that era. I think Alice, in many ways, she's kinda like, I mean, clearly she's a woman, but kind of genderless in terms of interests and capacity...it's almost like gender didn't have anything to do with it.

ANNE BURKHOLDER: She's just a very strong woman. Strong and with a big heart and with perseverance and endurance. And very intelligent. The big heart is the best thing of all.

DOUG DITTMAN: It's like...it's hard to be that person, to be that capable, and I think she just *had* to go right to the top. Because you just couldn't

stop her. She's just kind of like a force of nature. I've just started *maybe* having an upper hand in ping pong. She is a fierce competitor.

[on screen: ALICE when grandson misses the table on his volley, "That's okay. I like that."]

ANNE BURKHOLDER: I'm not taking her on in ping pong. Ever.

DOUG DITTMAN: To this day, if you're going to take her on in ping pong, you have to completely focus and put all your effort into it and just be kind of ruthless to win. (laughs) But she expects that, and she would not be satisfied with anything less. She's fearless, to this day, it's like, 'oh my gosh, where's she gonna drive to?' You know?

NARRATOR: Alice has thrived on the 'road less traveled'.

JOHN DITTMAN: Mom, how was your ping pong match?

ALICE: It was great. Your son did so well but I almost beat him.

ANNE BURKHOLDER: (looking at landscape art) The far distant horizon represents the future, like 'where are you going', or 'what is your horizon'. 'How are you going to get there?' 'What road are you going to pick?' So some of my paintings are representative of 'where are you going', 'what are you seeing off in the distance', 'what are you planning out there'. I think that same thing happens to Alice, though I don't know that she puts it in those kinds of words, but I think she's always looking for something new to do. She's not just sitting there spinning her wheels, she's always looking at the future.

DOUG DITTMAN: I really don't know what created Alice. I really don't. Like I said, I think it's just like a bolt of lightning. I'm really glad she was able to express her unique abilities in the world. She is the kind of person who smashes through barriers. I'm really glad that she was that person and able to do that, and that she encouraged so many other women.

ALICE: Opportunities are there if you look for them. That's what I'm trying to instill in the grandkids. So far I'm doing well. ¤

"Dittman is a born improver, one of those people who pick up an object and ask how it could look better, run better, be better."
AMERICAN BANKERS MAGAZINE

I think the clipping on the next page is one of the best articles to inspire growth, even if it is almost 28 years old. In the background of the photo is Steve Lindgren, a valued leader at Cornhusker Bank. ▶

Banker positive about future of finance

ALICE DITTMAN:

There are 373 banks in the state now. That is a declining number because more and more independent institutions are being taken over as part of chains, or, in the case of Vistar Bank, as part of a strong Midwestern chain, Norwest. So, the independence factor is diminishing a little bit.

But I feel positive about our future in the industry in our ability to adapt to a changing environment. Forty percent of our numbers of transactions now, instead of being teller-driven, are through the electronic media: ACH (Automated Clearing House) or ATM (Automated Teller Machine). It's a strong figure. It surprises me. It's up from 33 percent the year before.

Our bank is aggressive in that way. We have 18 ATMs around town. We're able to service those with one person. ACH transactions are things such as government checks and Railroad Retirement checks. What used to be checks are now electronic impulses. It's printed on customers' statement, the source is listed, but there's no paper.

The customer the benefit of knowing that the funds are there at the earliest possible moment. It's a very safe, secure feeling to have the credit being made on a certain day of the month.

Without fail, it eliminates some of the hazards — like losing a check, failing to endorse it, having someone else endorse it. It's voluntary. The federal government encourages it; it lessens their burden, their overhead. It's part of their effort towards efficiency. . . .

Let's face it, we're in a real struggle as an industry to keep our costs down. Added volume in a more efficient manner, certainly. Our drive-in tellers will do 50 percent more transactions in a day than a lobby teller.

We balance that out in our bank by having other responsibilities for lobby tellers. But people love the drive-in on days when it's 7 degrees below zero, not having to get out of their car. If we can match up what suits the customer and at the same time enhance our effectiveness, that's what we have to do.

In the old days, you were a teller, deposit gatherer and loan processor in the morning. At 2 p.m. you became a bookkeeper; you did the books after the lobby door closed. You had to wear two hats. It took a long time to get all those entries posted.

Originally, they had to be posted manually in a Boston ledger, a big bound leather volume. Every customer had a page. We'd post their checks, their deposits, and add it all up. We still have our original Boston ledger from our bank's origins back in 1903.

We evolved using machines. Now electronic capability is just all transmitted over a little wire.

Frustrations from the feds

(Coping with such regulations as indoor air and disabilities acts is) minor compared to some of the frustrations caused by overregulation of banks.

Like a customer said, they would like a loan and they would like their money by Friday, and it happened to be secured by real estate. No way can we do that and comply with the regulations. No way. It's not a matter of just drawing up a note, and taking a mortgage and checking the filings like we used to do. . . .

For example, there's a three-day right of recision. In certain situations, you have to close for flood plain. Just getting an appraiser is time-consuming. We wouldn't quote less than 30 days. On some houses over $100,000, days. Customers don't have to be

Alice Dittman is president and chairman of Cornhusker Bank.

urging us to get a third party to do the appraisal. I don't think that's really necessary.

New imaging

Our bank is considering going into imaging. Nobody does it yet here in town, but it's becoming very commonplace in other areas of the country.

Imaging is returning not the checks but an image of the checks. Customers don't have to do carbon checks, and they get their choice of image numbers on a page, from 9 to 48. The image page shows the checks in numerical sequence with the date they were paid. Customers don't have to

shuffle checks and reorganize them. . . .

The thing that I really love is we send out the imprints on three-ring punch paper. You could take your whole year's statement on a three-ring binder to your accountant, all neat, your storage problems minimized, and the IRS accepts it.

If you ever need an endorsement, it's available on microfilm, like it always has been. . . .

It's brand new technology. Our savings is primarily in the postage and the filing of the documents. That will enable us to offer this to our customers at the same cost that we've been

charging forever. We feel it's a real enhancement. It's coming. Miniaturization is unbelievable!

The other thing that is in the future is the retrieval of information. That is what banking is all about. We don't have a product to sell; we just have a service. Our effectiveness in being able to retrieve that information is really crucial to our success.

We microfilm — everybody microfilms — but now our main resource for retrieval of our bank information and our customers' information is on optic disk. On one side of an optic disk — no bigger than my hand, ¼ inch, I think — we can store 8,000 checking

accounts or 12 statements a year. One side of one disk. It's fantastic. The miniaturization — it's unbelievable.

When I came back to the bank in 1975 we had 27 employees per million (dollars) in deposits. As of year end, we're .8 of an employee per million. That's what all the enhancements and mechanical changes have done. And I think with absolutely the same level of service to our customers, in fact better, because our retrieval time is better than it was.

Emphasis on education

You commented about the diminishing numbers of middle management. I think that is definitely true. I would almost say, though, what were considered to be the more entry-level positions — and still are entry-level perhaps — are being enhanced more up to what a beginning manager role was. I see that continuing with more emphasis on education for our staff.

We've signed up for Sky Link. This is a service that the American Bankers Association puts out. Every Tuesday morning from 5 a.m. to 7 a.m., they transmit two hours of programming to our bank, taken in by a satellite dish which we've had installed on the roof of our building. It's not an inexpensive service, but it's the one way that I am going to be able to educate a much greater number of our employees to banking techniques, management techniques and changing regulations.

Banking on excitement

Every day a new challenge. I always say banking is the most exciting field you could choose, because every day is different, and you can make a difference in people's lives. There isn't any other job I could have done that would have permitted me to do that.

Conference: Five to enter Hall of Fame; Tri-Faith Initiative to receive Summit Award

Continued from Page 1

clude Ryan Severino, a New York economist who will talk about the national market and "Where does Nebraska fit in?"

Workshops will focus on topics including the "epic war on talent," and forces behind rapid hotel growth and high construction costs.

Individuals and projects that have made an imprint on the local landscape will be recognized, too.

Five people to be inducted into the CRE Summit Hall of Fame: Laura Alley, business development director at Alley Poyner Macchietto Architecture; Alice Dittman, retired chief executive and president of Cornhusker Bank; Doug Halvorson, lead landscape architect at Olsson engineering; John J. Hughes, awarded posthumously, broker at Dial Capital; and Jim

| Alice Dittman | John J. Hughes | Jim Maenner | Laura Alley | Doug Halvorson |

Maenner, vice president of CBRE Real Estate.

The Tri-Faith Initiative is to receive the Summit Award for shining positive light on Omaha, Slusky said. The project's Christian church, Jewish synagogue and Muslim mosque share a campus at Sterling Ridge off 132nd and Pacific Streets and are acclaimed as a standout example of interfaith cooperation.

The "Deal of the Year" will go to those involved with securing

a new home for LinkedIn at Sterling Ridge. Under construction is a 200,000-square-foot complex the tech company will lease.

"Development of the Year" (for the Omaha area) goes to Lockwood Development for the overall Sterling Ridge redevelopment project. For Lincoln, the winning team paved the way for the Scheels store at SouthPointe Pavilions.

For more information on the conference, go to https://www.attendcresummit.com/.

I can always find time to catch up with friends like Anne Burkholder whose dreams are now a well-established reality.

Cornhusker Bank breaking ground at 84th and O

Building at 11th and Cornhusker to stay open.

Lincoln Journal Star

Courtesy image

Cornhusker Bank plans to start building a four-story corporate headquarters at 84th and O streets on Friday. This is a rendering of what it will look like, looking northwest from O Street.

Cornhusker Bank will break ground for its new $13 million corporate center at 8310 O St. on Friday morning.

Cornhusker Bank Chairman John Dittman and CEO Barry Lockard will preside over the ceremony for invited guests to start construction of the 55,000-square-foot building. Mayor Chris Beutler will be speaking, along with Wendy Birdsall, president of the Lincoln Chamber of Commerce.

The bank filed a building permit for the construction on Monday. It will be oriented toward O Street, west of the Aldi's store at 84th Street, and east of Russwood Parkway. Parking will be north of the bank.

Lockard showed images and plans for the limestone building during a City Council meeting earlier this year.

Building the corporate center at 84th and O, identified as a growth area and city entryway by city planners, made a lot of sense, he said. It allows the bank to have a visual presence at a key location and provides convenience for customers.

"We are making an investment in this building, understanding this is an entryway into Lincoln," Lockard told the council.

The city waived height limitations to allow the four-story building on the northwest corner, as recommended by the Lincoln-Lancaster County Planning Commission.

Lincoln is the bank's home and marketplace. The bank moved from Davey to Lincoln in 1960. The existing corporate headquarters at 11th Street and Cornhusker Highway will remain open and a part of the business.

The new corporate center will include a 2,500-square-foot community room that can be used by customers, clients and employees, a way to share with the community, Lockard told the City Council.

The bank also plans to build a 2,000-square-foot commercial building on a small lot north of Aldi's, at the corner of 84th Street and College Park Drive, to be leased to an operator. "Something along the lines of food," Lockard said. That is still in the planning stages.

Cornhusker Bank expects to move into its new corporate center during mid-summer 2016.

Sampson Construction is the general contractor. Sinclair Hille is the architect.

RANDY HAMPTON/LINCOLN JOURNAL

Alice Dittman, president of Cornhusker Bank and new head of the Lincoln Chamber of Commerce, keeps an eye on Lincoln through her telescope.

Dittman says downtown problems are responsibility of all Lincolnites

BY GENE KELLY - JOURNAL WRITER

Alice Dittman likes to think that her perspective on Lincoln's problems and potential is a bit different from most.

"Some people look at the task of revitalizing downtown Lincoln the same way they would face digging out from a snowstorm. But I try to view problems as opportunities," she said. "The downtown is a challenge we all have to buy into. It is the downtown that needs more of our attention right now than other parts of the city. A parent tries to love all of his children equally, but he must give more attention to the one who needs it the most. We must do the same with downtown Lincoln."

Dittman's time will be balanced this year between her role as suburban banker and the top leadership position with the Lincoln Chamber of Commerce.

She is the first woman elected to head the chamber. She has been president of Cornhusker Bank since 1975.

Since she moved to an apartment high in Sky Park Manor at 13th and J streets, near the Capitol, she marvels at the "magnificent sunsets" to be seen through her telescope.

"I would stack that view up against any mountains or seashore I've seen," she said.

LINCOLN JOURNAL - FEBRUARY 19, 1988

From her balcony, a new telescope brings the panorama of Lincoln close.

"Lincoln looks so very different each day," she said. "I can see down O Street, into the auto dealerships, and north all the way to Belmont."

She decided to sell her home and move downtown when her cat died.

"It all happened rather quickly after this apartment became available. Getting to 7:15 a.m. meetings involving chamber committees is certainly easier this way," she said.

Dittman became active in the chamber because "each generation has to assume responsibility" for the one that follows.

"Why am I boosting Lincoln? Its quality of life won't stay this way if we don't," she said. "Those of us who are high on Lincoln and feel good about the community, its schools and government need to say so."

Dittman was born in Lincoln. She says that although some residents may complain about the adversities of winter, "it is the four seasons that add zest" to the quality of life. "The cycles of change bring a renewal of life each year. It's not by accident that Nebraskans live longer. We're a hardy people, more self-sufficient."

The chamber's 1,700 members represent about a third of the businesses in the city.

"These folks pay their dues because the organization provides services they often can't do for themselves" she said, "like lobbying for legislation, attending City Council meetings and reviewing the city budget. A chamber functions as a gathering point for local facts and figures."

Dittman agrees with people who say the chamber must attract more manufacturing jobs.

"We are the host city of the state. There must be a focus on creating the type of jobs that will give displaced farm families an alternative to leaving the state. A community that wants to grow must go out and ask for business," she said.

Is Lincoln's low unemployment rate really a negative factor in trying to attract manufacturing jobs?

"I don't accept that premise," Dittman said. "Many people would move back to Lincoln if the job opportunities existed."

She says the Midwest work ethic is alive and well.

"Most of us are not too far from our agricultural roots. If something is broken, we'll fix it or locate someone who can."

She is bothered by the outmigration of Nebraska's young people.

"These are the folks who are innovative and adapt easily to change. We must not lose them," she said.

Retention of jobs by Nebraska employers has been one of the main results of LB775 during the first year the economic development law has been in effect, she said, and "now we must use this tool to give priority to wider job creation."

Dittman is a staunch backer of good schools and teachers.

"They cost money, but mediocrity is not enough," she said. ¤

Nebraska Grandmother Blazes Trails in Running Family's Cornhusker Bank

BRONSTIEN, BARBARA F., AMERICAN BANKER

LINCOLN, Neb. -- When Alice M. Dittman's husband died 19 years ago, she suddenly became the provider for three teenage children.

"I set out to try and maintain a standard of living for myself and my kids that they would have had if their father had still been alive," she says.

So, Mrs. Dittman, a banker's daughter with two business degrees and plenty of banking experience herself, went back to work full time for her father's Cornhusker Bank - as president and chief executive.

Since then Mrs. Dittman - now a white-haired, 63-year-old grandmother of two - has made a name for herself in Lincoln.

She was the first woman to head the Nebraska Bankers Association, in 1993-94, and the first to crack such all-male preserves as the board of the Country Club of Lincoln.

"Alice is an absolutely tremendous role model for women," said James A. Mastera, Cornhusker's executive vice president. "But more than that, Alice is a tremendous role model for both men and women, I don't think she's striving to be a pioneer. She's striving to succeed, and as a result of that, these things occur."

Earlier this year, her $109 million-asset bank became the first in Nebraska to do check imaging. It also was the first in this city of 200,000 to have a minority board member, in 1991.

It became the first Lincoln bank to offer 24-hour phone access to accounts three years ago, when it introduced "Call the Kernel." The service averages 272 calls a day.

"The others got in line pretty quickly after that," Mrs. Dittman said. "They just couldn't take the competition."

Mrs. Dittman's banking strategy is to grow Cornhusker 10% or more per year and be in the top 25% nationally with return on assets. Its ratio was at 1.61% at yearend 1993.

"This is the first six months in 19 years that I've been president that we have shown no growth," said Mrs. Dittman, who is now chairman as well. The problem for her own and other area banks might be the popularity of alternative investments amid recent low interest rates; she said.

Looking ahead, she'd like to add a Cornhusker branch on the city's southwest side to the bank's five current locations.

But she's not too interested in acquiring community banks in other areas, saying: "I have not been very aggressive on that simply because I have felt rather than to buy an $8 [million] or $9 million bank, why not just grow another $8 [million] or $9 million and not have to pay a premium?" And Mrs. Dittman, who plays tennis each week, golfs and was certified in scuba diving last November, has no plans to slow down herself just yet.

An avid traveler who hit six continents in 1992, Ms. Dittman said she'll maintain her current positions for a couple years and remain on the bank's board until age 70. "I think you can stay too long," she said. "When you start phasing down, you're no longer as effective."

However, Mrs. Dittman, whose family continues to control the bank's ownership, and whose son John became a vice president this summer, doesn't intend to sell.

"I think having John come back makes

that statement," she said. "We've put together too good a staff here to have that destroyed."

Her father, George A. Frampton, bought the bank's predecessor, Farmers State Bank, Davey, Neb., in 1948.

Mrs. Dittman, who holds a bachelor's degree in business administration and a master's in finance and management from the University of Nebraska, worked in Davey as cashier from 1953 to 1959.

In 1960, Mr. Frampton moved the bank 12 miles south to Lincoln and changed its name.

Meanwhile, Mrs. Dittman and her husband, Marcus, worked at a start-up, Central Bank in Central City, Neb., from 1959 to 1964; and in 1965 they helped set up another de novo, First National Bank, Richmond, Mo.

During the next 10 years, while her husband served as president of the Missouri bank, Mrs. Dittman mainly raised their three children. She also worked part time for Cornhusker Bank and served on its board.

After her husband died, she returned to Lincoln and became Cornhusker's president and chief executive, titles her father relinquished to become chairman.

"When I came back to Lincoln in 1975, a lot of people didn't know me," she said.

Thus, she began to lay the groundwork for acceptance among her male peers.

"I'd go to a meeting and there may be a hundred people there, three or four of which were women," Mrs. Dittman said. "The easy thing would have been to go and visit with the three or four women. I didn't let myself do that."

No one has outright opposed her in any of her endeavors because she is a woman. "I never get negative feedback," she said. "You don't. It's just being ignored that's probably the most tangible way that women are kept 'in their place.'"

She also didn't let herself be rendered

extinct in 1981, when a San Francisco Chronicle columnist wrote during an American Bankers Association convention that since there would be no need for small banks under deregulation, community bankers were unlikely to be back when the conference returned to San Francisco five years later. He cited Mrs. Dittman in particular, probably because she was on the ABA board.

But by 1986, Cornhusker had doubled in size, and Ms. Dittman let the columnist know her bank was alive and well and that she was headed back west. This time, the column was headlined, "Alice M. Dittman Makes It Back to S.F. Again."

Mrs. Dittman "usually has an opinion about a lot of things and is not afraid to express it," said James A. Hansen, director of Nebraska's Department of Banking and Finance. "She's full of new ideas and thoughtful perspective."

Some of her pet projects around town have included advising Lincoln's new Small Business Resource Center and soliciting funds to more an old bank building to a turn-of-the-century "Main Street" at Nebraska's fairgrounds. She also helped to develop a new banking exhibit at the local children's museum.

What would her husband have thought of all her accomplishments? "He would have done all these things too if he would have been here," she said. "I'm sure he'd be very pleased."¤

Questia, a part of Gale, Cengage Learning. www.questia.com. Article title: Nebraska Grandmother Blazes Trails in Running Family's Cornhusker Bank. Contributors: Bronstien, Barbara F. - Author. Magazine title: American Banker. Volume: 159. Issue: 171 Publication date: September 6, 1994. Page number: 7. © SourceMedia Inc. COPYRIGHT 1994 Gale Group.

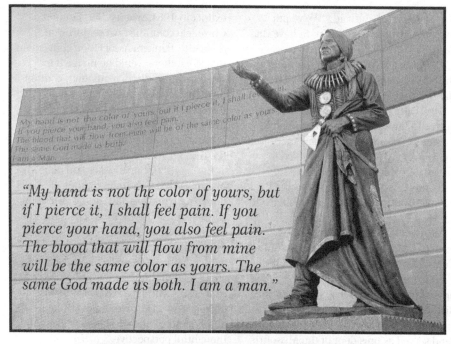

"My hand is not the color of yours, but if I pierce it, I shall feel pain. If you pierce your hand, you also feel pain. The blood that will flow from mine will be the same color as yours. The same God made us both. I am a man."

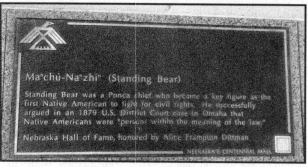

Ma"chú-Na"zhí" (Standing Bear)

Standing Bear was a Ponca chief who became a key figure as the first Native American to fight for civil rights. He successfully argued in an 1879 U.S. District Court case in Omaha that Native Americans were "persons within the meaning of the law."

Nebraska Hall of Fame, honored by Alice Frampton Dittman

NEBRASKA'S CENTENNIAL MALL

I find that most people are moved when they read the eloquent words spoken in an Omaha U.S. District Court by Ponca Chief Standing Bear. And so am I, which makes me grateful to have had a small part in honoring his legacy in a permanent space on Lincoln's Centennial Mall.

SCULPTOR BEN VICTOR HAS GIVEN US THIS
NEBRASKA TREASURE.

I've always said,
"Things fade and rust,
but the real value is in
relationships with people."

★

"Enthusiasm," I like to say, "is essential to success.
Nothing great is ever achieved without enthusiasm.
If you or the people you work with don't have
enthusiasm, the odds of success are greatly
diminished."

RECOGNITIONS, AWARDS, AND BOARDS

Beta Gamma Sigma Business Administration Honorary		1952
P.E.O. Chapter AB, Central City, NE	President	1962
Peoples Natural Gas Board of Directors		1964
PTA, Richmond, Missouri	President	1968
Winding River Girl Scout Council, Kansas City, MO	President	1971-75
NETS Nebraska Electronic Transfer System	Board of Directors	1977-86
Nebraska Wesleyan University Board of Governors		1976-79
Nebraska Wesleyan University Distinguished Service Award		1979
University of Nebraska President's Advisory Committee		1979-1993
St. Paul United Methodist Church Finance Committee		1980-Present
Lincoln High School Distinguished Alumni in Business		1980
American Bankers Association Board of Directors Leadership Council		1980-82
Bryan Hospital Board of Trustees		1980-84
Bryan Hospital Board of Trustees	Chairman	1982-84
Alpha Xi Delta Sorority Edna Epperson Brinkman Award		1981
NETS Nebraska Electronic Transfer System	President	1983-86
Nebraska Independent College Foundation Board of Trustees		1984-88
Nebraska Bankers Association Executive Council		1985-88
American Bankers Association Fund for Economic Education Board		1987-90
Phi Chi Theta, U of N Business Woman of the Year		1987
NBISCO Nebraska Bankers Insurance and Services Corporation		1987-88
Lincoln Chamber of Commerce Board of Directors		1985-89
Lincoln Chamber of Commerce	President	1988
Nebraska State Chamber of Commerce		1988-to retirement
University of Nebraska - Nebraska Builders Award		1989
University of Nebraska Chancellors Club		
National Guard Association Distinguished Service Award		1989
Small Business Association Women in Business Advocate		1989
Lincoln Jaycees CEO Community Service Award		1990
LIBA Lincoln Independent Business Association Business of the Year		1991

Recognitions, Awards, and Boards
continued

UNL College of Business Administration Business Leadership Award		1991
YWCA Co-Chair Capital Campaign		1991
Nebraska State Chamber of Commerce	Chairman	1992
NBISCO Nebraska Bankers Insurance and Services Corporation		1992-96
Nebraska Bankers Association Executive Council		1992-96
Nebraska Bankers Association Executive Council	President	1993-94
Belmont Elementary School Lifetime Member PTA		1993
Arthritis Foundation Woman of the Year - Lincoln		1993
Country Club of Lincoln Board of Directors		1993-1997
Governors CEO Roundtable Enhancing Global Opportunities		1994
Rotary Nebraskan of the Year	(First female)	1994
Nebraskaland Foundation Pioneer Award		1994
UNL College of Business Administration Entrepreneur of the Year		1995
FFA Agriculture Leadership		1996
Doane College President's Award for Leadership/Commencement Address		1996
UNL College of Business Administration Lifetime Honorary Membership		1996
Nebraska State Chamber of Commerce Business Hall of Fame		1996
Delta Sigma Pi Women's Business Fraternity Appreciation Award		1997
Kiwanis Club of Lincoln Distinguished Service Award		2001
UNL Alumni Honor Award		2002
Nebraska Bankers Association Fifty Year Banker Award		2003
Ribbon Medallion University of Nebraska Master Week Award		2004
Chamber of Commerce Burnham-Yates Award		2004
United Way of Lincoln & Lancaster County Women in Philanthropy Founders Award		2005
Aksarben Court of Honor		2009
Honorary Doctor of Laws - Nebraska Wesleyan University		2014
University of Nebraska Pathbreakers		2015
Lincoln Journal-Star INSPIRE Woman of the Year		2019
Commercial Real Estate Hall of Fame		2020

I was initiated into my mother's P.E.O. Chapter AI in 1949 at the age of 18. Here we all are in 2018 celebrating each other at The Landing. I'm proud and grateful to have belonged to this philanthropic educational organization for over 72 years now. P.E.O.'s leadership in providing scholarships and loans to deserving women is dear to my heart. [SEE WWW.PEOINTERNATIONAL.ORG.]

Dittman ... "It's very satisfying to know that our bank is perceived to be a caring partner in the community."

Elder Statesman of Lincoln Business

On golf, business or life, Alice Dittman still puts it straight and down the middle

State Chamber President Jack Swartz with Governor Ben Nelson at a proclamation signing in the Capitol when I was State Chamber Chairperson in 1992.

A message to my grandchildren

So many people I've watched over the years
have it in them to break new ground, to test
the limits of their abilities, and yet many have
not taken the first steps.

Why not? What do they have to lose?
What does a person gain by playing it safe?

Set a pace for yourself, have expectations,
gather mentors. Look for the stepping stones
and plant some of your own.

Once that pace builds momentum, there are
ceilings to be broken, pathways to be forged,
and lives to be changed.

Love,

Ganya

ACKNOWLEDGEMENTS

Many thanks to Penny Costello for sharing scanned photos and video transcriptions; Teresa Elliott for assistance with bank archives; UNL Writing and Photography coordinator Garrett Stolz; Kara Heideman, Director of Communications for the Nebraska Bankers Association; Craig Chandler, Director of Photography, Office of University Communications; Mary Weixelman, Lincoln Journal-Star media archival; Lovell Moser and Linda Ingram Hoegemeyer for editorial and proofing input; and in particular Mary Schwaner, whose vision for this project has taken it to heights I had not anticipated.

To those surprised to find your names in this book, please accept my belated request to solicit your permission.

Made in the USA
Monee, IL
10 February 2024

53217432R10125